Prison

of Culture

John Howard Griffin, 1959, preparing himself
for the "journey through the South" that would
change both himself and America.
Photograph by Don Rutledge.

John Howard Griffin

Prison
of Culture

Beyond *Black Like Me*

Edited by Robert Bonazzi

With a Remembrance by Studs Terkel

WingsPress

San Antonio, Texas
2011

Prison of Culture: Beyond Black Like Me © 2011
by The Estate of John Howard Griffin and Elizabeth Griffin-
Bonazzi. See acknowledgments for publication histories of individual
essays. Introduction © 2011 by Robert Bonazzi. All rights reserved.

First Edition, 2011

Print Edition ISBN: 978-0-916727-82-6
ePub ISBN: 978-1-60940-147-4
Kindle ISBN: 978-1-60940-148-1
Library PDF ISBN: 978-1-60940-149-8

Wings Press
627 E. Guenther • San Antonio, Texas 78210
Phone/fax: (210) 271-7805 • www.wingspress.com
Distributed by Independent Publishers Group • www.ipgbook.com

Library of Congress Cataloging-in-Publication data:

Griffin, John Howard, 1920-1980.
 Prison of culture : beyond Black like me / John Howard Griffin ; edited by
Robert Bonazzi ; with a preface by Studs Terkel. -- 1st ed.
  p. cm.
 Includes bibliographical references.
 ISBN 978-0-916727-82-6 (pbk., printed edition : alk. paper) -- ISBN 978-
1-60940-147-4 (epub ebook) -- ISBN 978-1-60940-148-1 (kindle ebook)
-- ISBN 978-1-60940-149-8 (library pdf ebook)
 1. United States--Race relations. 2. Discrimination--United States. 3.
Stereotypes (Social psychology)--United States. 4. Prejudices--United
States. 5. Racism--United States. 6. Spirituality. I. Bonazzi, Robert. II.
Terkel, Studs, 1912- III. Title.
 E185.615.G73 2011
 305.800973--dc23
                              2011019450

Contents

A Remembrance   ix
    by Studs Terkel

Introduction: Beyond *Black Like Me*   xi
    by Robert Bonazzi

I. Essays on Racism

Privacy of Conscience   3
The Intrinsic *Other*   9
Profile of a Racist   13
On *Killers of the Dream*   14
Requiem for A Martyr   18
Racist Sins of Christians   22
Malcolm X   35
American Racism in the Sixties   51
From *A Time To Be Human*   68

II. Essays on Spirituality

Poulenc Behind the Mask   85
Fraternal Dialogue   92
The Little Brothers   102
The Terrain of Physical Pain   109
Final Reflections   118

Acknowledgments   126
About the Editor   129

To the Memory of
Studs Terkel

A Remembrance

Griffin never failed to astonish. It was his capacity to go beyond himself.

He suffered more ills than any man should be heir to—you name it, he had it.

Let's not even talk about that awful beating he took in the kidneys when the Klan caught up with him along some southern dirt road. When he died, his wife Elizabeth said it was of "everything."

But he had endured so long because he was possessed by the *Other*.

When he transformed himself in *Black Like Me*, he was responding to the challenge: To wake up some morning in the oppressed's skin. To think human rather than *white*. To *feel* human. Feeling, as much as understanding, is what he was all about.

In his empathy for the *Other*, he understood the tragedy of the child who belongs to the "oppressor" species, living in darkness. The Klansman's kid, the Nazi's child, the bigot's offspring. It was this "dying of the light" he most raged against.

During my last visit, he lay on his dying bed. He despaired of the mindless official optimism and the unofficial cynicism and yet he clung to the slender reed of hope. "Life is a risk," Griffin told me during our last visit. "And what a horror if you don't face those risks. If you don't, you end up being utterly paralyzed. You don't ever do anything."

I can't help but reflect on the other roads this gifted man might have traveled had he not been possessed by the *Other*. Several literary critics have conjectured that had John Howard Griffin been less committed, he might have become an important American novelist. As matters stand, he was merely an important human being.

Let's settle for that.

Studs Terkel
Chicago, 1980

A mind enclosed in language is in prison.

—Simone Weil (1909-1943)

He who establishes his argument by noise and command shows that his reason is weak.

—Michel de Montaigne (1533-1592)

Take the teaching of logic out of a civilization and reason is reduced to the squalor of prejudice. All of the classic fallacies of logic then become a sort of weird virtue and man seeks by loudness, fear and violence to win causes that could not be won by rational persuasion.

—John Howard Griffin, 1960

Introduction
Beyond *Black Like Me*

Robert Bonazzi

The Intrinsic *Other*

A central theme of *Prison of Culture*—that cultures tend to view other cultures as *intrinsically other,* as less developed versions of their presumed superior culture—was one of Griffin's core concepts. In his seminal essay ("The Intrinsic *Other*") he lucidly characterizes this inculcated attitude and clarifies the fallacies inherent in it.

Griffin writes: "One of the characteristics of our expression of such attitudes is that they are often perfectly natural to the speaker but unnatural to the hearer. They reveal in the speaker the falsity of viewing others as intrinsically *Other*, intrinsically different as men. This intrinsic difference always implies some degree of inferiority." These societal attitudes are taught directly by our in-group and absorbed indirectly from culture, imprisoning our perceptions within an unconscious code of prejudice.

In "The Intrinsic *Other*" Griffin cites the Irish jurist Edmund Burke for providing the logical and ethical "touchstone for this error when he said: 'I know of no way of drawing up an indictment against a whole people.' Racism begins when we draw up an indictment against a whole people merely by considering them as under-developed versions of ourselves, by perpetuating the blindness of the stereotype." Griffin emphasizes this point in the essay. "This is insidious because it is often done in good faith, is often accomplished with an illusion of benevolence. It leads to master delusion. The delusion lies in the fact that no matter how well we think we know the *Other*, we still judge from within the imprisoning framework of our own limited cultural criteria, we still speak within the cliché of the stereotype."

For Griffin there was no *intrinsic Other*. He perceived only extrinsic differences among individuals in stark contrast to the essential commonalities of all human beings. "The illusion of the *Other*, of these superficial differences, is deeply imbedded through this inculcated stereotype we make of the *Other*, which falsifies man's view of man. I believe that before we can truly dialogue in depth, we must first perceive that there is no *Other*, that the *Other* is oneself in all essentials."

Since 2003, as revealed by the Human Genome Project, we now know "that the *Other* is oneself in all essentials." While every human being has a unique DNA sequence that differs from every other person on the planet, we differ from each other by just 0.1%, regardless of ethnic origin. All humans are 99.9% the same, and therefore "race" is *not* a biological reality but merely a cultural phenomenon based on prejudice.

"Profile of A Racist" is a brief typology of racists. The first type "feels he has the duty to indulge" in violence and murder "for the good of society"—the type we associate with the Ku Klux Klan or the Gestapo. But it is the second type who gets overlooked, the one who metaphorically "weaves the lynch rope that he himself would not use," keeping silent about routine injustices and denying any prejudice, because this type was the direct beneficiary of the segregated system.

In Germany this "second type" kept silent about the extermination of the Jews, and the pattern of madness led to the genocide of the European Jewish community, to the *de facto* enslavement of the segregated African American minority in the Deep South, and to the ultimate dehumanization of society. Griffin first realized the tragic truth of this process, refined to hideous perfection, when as a student in France he worked in the resistance movement. Hitler had drawn up an anti-Semitic indictment against the Jewish people, blaming his victims for every real or imagined problem in Germany.

In *A Time To Be Human* (1977), Griffin looks back on the Jewish families he befriended and hid away in the alley boarding houses of Tours, France. It was in those rooms that Jewish parents, realizing that eventually they would be captured and shipped to concentration camps, asked him and his French friends in the *Defense Passive* to take their children to safety. Near the end of this reflection, he makes the connection between those boarding house rooms and the shanty rooms of the Deep South, where he witnessed the same grief on the faces of black parents who had lost their children to white racist violence.

"Requiem for A Martyr" (1964) tells such a story. Clyde Kennard was framed for a petty crime and sentenced to seven years of hard labor, because he was the first black person to register at a segregated college in Mississippi. Kennard had been a paratrooper in Korea, an honors scholar at the University of Chicago, and a tax-paying citizen in the county where the college was located. Yet his peaceful actions were considered an attack upon segregation.

The Christ Ideal

When asked how he could advocate breaking some laws while obeying others, Dr. Martin Luther King, Jr. responded: "The answer is found in the fact that there are two types of laws. There are *just* and *unjust* laws. I would agree with St. Augustine that 'An unjust law is no law at all.'" His sources of wisdom were not only to be found in the work of Thoreau, but he had also studied the example of Gandhi's creed of nonviolence. Gandhi had revered Christ as the ultimate figure to have "offered himself as a sacrifice for the good of others, including his enemies, and became the ransom of the world." In King's magnificent text to clergymen in 1963, *Letter from a Birmingham Jail,* he offered several astute arguments about justice and the law.

> A just law is a man-made code that squares with the moral law or law of God. An unjust law is a code that is out of harmony with the moral law. Any law that

uplifts human personality is just. Any law that degrades human personality is unjust. . . . An unjust law is a code that a majority inflicts on a minority that is not binding on itself. . . . All segregation statutes are unjust because segregation distorts the soul and damages the personality. It gives the segregator a false sense of superiority, and the segregated a false sense of inferiority. . . segregation is not only politically, economically and sociologically unsound, but it is morally wrong and sinful. . . .So I urge men to disobey segregation ordinances because they are morally wrong.

King then placed these reflections into a context of Christian theology for his fellow clergymen in order to reveal his nonviolent intent. "In no sense," he points out, "do I advocate evading or defying the law as a rabid segregationist would do. This would lead to anarchy. One who breaks an unjust law must do it openly, lovingly . . . and with a willingness to accept the penalty." Breaking a law because one's conscience determines it to be unjust was for King "expressing the highest respect for law."

Gandhi wrote that "an unjust law is a species of violence," and "the law of nonviolence says that violence should not be resisted by counter-violence but by nonviolence." Both men endured imprisonment willingly and were prepared to die for the Christ ideal. Gandhi considered Christ's crucifixion "a perfect act of Charity."

In a Griffin essay about the Montgomery bus boycott, for *Ramparts* magazine, he stated King's challenge:

King's first problem was to inspire his people not only to persevere in their battle for freedom but to limit themselves to a single weapon—the weapon of Love: to return love for hate; to embrace a truth strange to modern ears but which black people's lives had uniquely prepared them to understand—*that unearned suffering is redemptive.* He asked fifty thousand people to do that rare thing—to make themselves subservient to an ideal (the Christ Ideal) in the face of opponents who made ideals subservient to their prejudices. His second problem was to place the Christ Ideal in firm opposition to segregationists, who were persuaded that they themselves acted from the noblest Christian motives and felt it wholly within the framework of Christianity to smear, terrorize, kill or do anything else to protect the traditional Southern Christian System from anyone who sought to alter it.

The fraternal love ethic of Christ and Thoreau's *Essay on Civil Disobedience* were integral to Gandhi's nonviolent creed, which ended the occupation of the British in India, as well as to King's Christian values that eventually dismantled the segregated system in the Deep South. These peaceful resistance movements, led by two religious leaders committed to human rights for all, not only avoided most physical violence but also the "internal violence of the spirit," as King pointed out.

"Through physical attacks, jailings, framed-up assaults on his character, King continued to lead and inspire…" writes Griffin. "In the market place of harshest reality he proved his thesis: that the Christ Ideal is not only a valid way, but in the case of Montgomery, Alabama, was the *only* way to insure victory: that the highest idealism is the ultimate practicality."

The "Christ Ideal" was evident also in Lillian Smith's *Killers of the Dream*, an autobiographical account of a privileged white woman in Georgia. After Griffin reviewed the book, a fascinating correspondence between the two novelists began. When he read the new edition, he hastily typed "reactions directly" into his journal.

Lillian Smith seeks to recreate the southern experience in order to help both her fellow southerners and all men understand the tremendous forces that have grown into the southern white and led him to "Kill the Dream" of our founding fathers all in deluding himself that he is preserving something infinitely more precious—the South, segregation, southern womanhood. In order to show the tragic growth of all these forces, she writes a semi-autobiographical work, telling of her typical southern upbringing, the influences on childhood in a genteel southern family, the combined degradation of the South after the Civil War, and the assuagement they took in the only thing that could *not* be degraded—the white superiority of their skin (abetted by ruthless politicians and wealthy families). White supremacy became their firmest belief—the Negro became the "object" on which they could safely vent all of their hatreds and frustrations.

Griffin had not read the first edition of *Killers of the Dream* (1950), since he was blind at the time. He knew only Smith's first novel, *Strange Fruit*, which had a powerful effect on him as a teenager (and he mentions this in *Black Like Me*). The opening of the review differs from his journal: "Lillian Smith, as the whole world surely knows, is a Southern Lady. Twelve years ago, with prophetic vision she wrote *Killers of the Dream*, about the South and segregation." In his journal he notes he had read the book as "a magnificent free-form essay, one of those rare works that literally pours out from a mind that has pondered deeply and come to many conclusions without ever losing the passion she felt for her subject." The book had caused him to rediscover his abandoned roots, to "become a Southerner vicariously."

There are interesting corollaries between *Killers of the Dream* and *Black Like Me*. Their tones are boldly critical and, by natural turns, deeply compassionate—and both express undertones of naked vulnerability. They share aristocratic artistry and novelistic control, elevated beyond mere reportage. Both authors struggled with a sense of guilt and intended white readers to do the same. They had similar upbringings—Griffin's in Texas as a member of an educated family and Smith's in Georgia as "a member of a cultivated and respected family."

Their differences are complementary: Griffin's concern with the "manhood" of segregated black men and Smith's demystification of the white "Southern Lady." His breakthrough came with a return to the Deep South, while Smith's was accomplished without ever having left Georgia. They discovered spiritual affinities during a passionate correspondence. Their three-year dialogue—ended by Lillian Smith's death, at age 69, on September 28, 1966—produced 80 typewritten pages between them.

In the review, Griffin examines the southern white's rationalization of segregation through the eyes of Smith's courageous stand for justice and equality. She speaks of her parents, "who so gravely taught me to split my body from my mind and both from my 'soul,' taught me also to split my conscience from my acts and Christianity from southern tradition." Griffin's scathing remarks about southerners go beyond the refinement of Smith's viewpoint, in both defending her position and extending his critique to the central issue of sexuality (about which she only hinted). Griffin writes:

> The southern girls learned other things—a puritanical crushed-violet concept of sex, kindness to the Negro, the superiority of whiteness. They learned that Christ appointed the southern white to care for the well-being of the southern Negro, and that segregation was the proper and Christian way to insure the happiness of both races. They learned that it was unkind to encourage the Negro beyond the barriers erected for his own good.
>
> Most important of all, they learned that a Southern White Woman is sacred—a sacred reality who must be protected from the lion that raged beneath the thin layer of domestication nurtured in the *black* by the *white*.
>
> Open the door to the Negro's cage and the lion would bound out to rape the white sacredness, to despoil it and outrage heaven . . . and also create a servant problem.
>
> The southern white woman had her flowers, her kitchen, her illusion of sacredness. And there was a certain beauty in all of this if she swallowed her frustrations at being cheated by the husband who had chivalrously guarded her sacredness by lavishing his brute masculinity on Negro women and saving only the gentle leftovers for his wife.

Griffin considered Lillian Smith to be too genteel to write caustically or to say much about the perverse totalitarian caste system of the South, which allowed white men to rape black women with relative impunity, even during the segregation era. But Smith realized "that the warped, distorted frame we put around every Negro child from birth is around every white child also . . . what cruelly shapes and cripples the personality of one is cruelly shaping and crippling the personality of the other."

Smith reached the same religious conclusion as Dr. King, believing that all humanity is sacred. She asked the challenging question: "Are we—the nation that first embarked on the high adventure of making a world fit for human beings to live in—about to destroy ourselves because we have killed our dream?" Finally Smith gives readers a warning: "Time has run out; we must right now adjust ourselves to the speed and quality of world events, world moods, world psychology or face probable extinction as a free nation."

In his journal Griffin laments that Smith had been typecast—"somehow dragged down as an artist by the fact that she has demonstrated her gifts so superbly on this one subject that the world does not get to read her on any other. She has written many essays that have nothing to do with her 'Mother-of-the-whole-damned-South role.'"

Smith wrote in her first letter to Griffin that *Killers of the Dream* was "a book written almost with my blood: afterward, I was desperately sad for a year. I couldn't throw it off: I saw more as I wrote than I had expected to see: it was a kind of year-long vision of what we really are." After publication of the first edition in 1950, Smith had gone on a book tour. "I was so overwhelmed with sadness that the effete New Yorkers couldn't take it. They had come to the books-and-authors luncheons to be amused. And there I was, like Kierkegaard, fearing and trembling."

Griffin responded: "It was the same with me—a sense of utter disbelief and then a sort of cosmic terror that we have stepped beyond the limits of absolvable sin. I have learned, like you, what it is to have the 'privilege' of being sneaked into the back doors of kindly, cowardly people. I did not want to send you *Black Like Me*, for I felt it would needlessly increase the pain of your own experience; and most of all I felt it unworthy of being read by you."

"Let me tell you how I feel about *Black Like Me*," Smith began:

> I read it at one sitting, of course; how could anyone do otherwise! I stopped once to make a pot of coffee; I needed

caffeine. I read on. I'd stop now and then and whisper, 'Dear God, how can You forgive us! You can't; we have sinned *in extremis*.' I knew this. But you pushed it straight into my heart. You know the difference in knowing about and knowing. And you chose to know: which meant you must experience it yourself. I shall never forget this personal confession of a special and valid experience. I still bleed from it.

The sheer cruelty of the Negro's everyday life! How wanton and terrible is white-imposed necessity (placed upon blacks) to search for a toilet, for a glass of water. I felt this: we white southerners do not deserve to live. We are a soft, sweet, terrible people; a worse people, in many ways, than the Nazis: at least they knew what they were doing. (Yes, they pretend today that they don't; but they do, and they knew then. But we — we chant our hymns, we call everybody honey and sweetie, oh God . . . we smile, sprinkle sugar, every day we sprinkle sugar on pus-filled wounds.)

Behind your story so terrible and true, one could feel, I could feel, a fine intelligence, a well informed mind as well as a well informed heart. And it made me want to know you. What you did was not only courageous, it was imaginative and intelligent. You chose to know: and then to write down what you knew. This to me, is wonderful stuff.

In a 1963 letter, Griffin said: "Will you not be offended if I tell you I sent out word to our discalced Carmelite convents and asked that you be made the object of a perpetual novena?" Smith responded: "I am almost too touched to write about it," and then explained why:

My Grandfather was Catholic; reared in a Quebec monastery to be a priest. Left before his final vows; came South, met Grandmother, married her, fought on the southern side but was always opposed to slavery, to radical cruelty, to stupidity. Some of Grandfather is in me; and always I've had a feeling for the rituals and the prayers — not the Church, itself, as an Establishment (not liking any establishments) but for the profound way it has met the human need for reaching inward in prayer, the human need for mystery, for reverence, for awe; the human need to be forever humbled by majesty and grace and love — and the unimaginable . . . I have doors in me and on the surface of me that never close to the Unknown—which I understand is the most important part of us mortals. And I am humbly grateful for the novenas.

Inevitably their dialogue glided along personal lines and, given the essentially spiritual views that had shaped their lives and work, all "subjects" eventually circled back to contemplation of the Divine Object. Their correspondence was imbued with a familial tenderness and a commitment to humanistic values. Both were astonished and pleased by their spiritual similarities. Griffin compared "the great excitement of this correspondence" to "finding a new piece of music that strikes one just right; the pure joy of it." But he saw one distinct difference between them and expressed it to her.

> You have kept what I could not keep. . . you have kept a brilliant ability to analyze and synthesize. I once had this to a high degree and it is almost completely gone now. Your passion has sharpened your intellectual powers with no sacrifice of spirit. It has turned you into an aristocrat (if I may use such a term) and it has done just the opposite to me, turned me into a peasant, a gross mentality. I feel the loss, but feel also that as I abuse everything, I should have eventually abused this gift of the intellect—I drifted from ice toward the flame; whereas you have superbly counterpointed the two, with no sacrifice of either. At least, if one cannot do as you have done, it is better to burn than to freeze, as most of our intellectuals have managed to do wherever they have been afraid to marry the intellect with the soul.

This was hardly the utterance of "a gross mentality" but a variation of Griffin's sense of unworthiness. He concluded: "My work is reduced to the extremity of showing how life must smell like bread and sound like Bach." This lovely poetic figure—accurate for he baked bread and loved Bach above all composers—laments that his life cannot be such a sublime distillation. Instead of the spiritual essences, he felt reduced to the extremities of social conflict.

Black Power

In a 1966 interview Griffin revealed that the most frequent question asked of him was the question he also considered to be the most irrelevant ("Privacy of Conscience"):

> After the publication of *Black Like Me*, everyone was after me to explain my motive for doing such a thing. In the first place, it was nobody's damned business what my motives were. There is no more respect for the privacy of conscience. I tell them simply, I don't want my children becoming racists. And that's a good enough answer, even though it's not the real answer. . . .

During that same interview, he discussed what he saw as the shortcomings of *Black Like Me*. Had he realized the book would have a readership beyond academic circles, he would have not limited the "experiment" to the South and he would have written "about the failure of the churches." He expressed this fully in the interview.

> I have been criticized for this, and it is a most valid criticism. I did not write about it for two reasons. First, I was so deeply shocked to be driven away from churches that would have welcomed me any time as a white man that I did not know how to handle this and I feared I might be committing an injustice to write about it without proper time to think about it.
>
> Second, in my naiveté, I was certain that as soon as these conditions were made known to church leadership, the matter would be corrected. Well, I made them known and was given only the most blatant kinds of rationalizations to justify them by the very leadership I had thought would bring corrective measures. When I saw that nothing was

going to be done, that the official church leadership was not going to rock any boats, I published a piece called "Racist Sins of Christians" in *Sign* magazine. In this I spoke of my own experiences of being driven from 'white churches'—of the insanity and confusion that assault a man after he has been driven from the "house of God" when he stands outside and listens as the voices within sing hymns. What this proved was that racism, when it goes unrepudiated, ends up contaminating all institutions, even our highest: our schools, libraries, hospitals and churches. And this is not only in the South. We have problems of racism in churches all over the country and in churches of all denominations—these are matters well known by most Negroes but hardly known at all by the white populace.

Radicalized by *Black Like Me*, Griffin wrote increasingly critical works on racism. He became an advocate of Black Power, but without giving up nonviolence. "For approximately a decade," he writes in *The Church and the Black Man* (1969),

> black Americans persevered in the dream of non-violent resistance. But its success always depends on the conversion of the hostile white force. An indication of the dehumanizing character of racism on racists themselves is surely found in this failure of love and redemptive suffering to cure the wounds of racism. Non-violent resistance appeared to have failed. In fact, racists redoubled their efforts in the name of patriotism and Christianity, to suppress not only black people but all non-racists.

However "nonviolence did, in fact, make profound changes in that it did touch and move many individuals; but these changes were intimate, surrounded by confusion, filled with fears of reprisals and character assassination." Griffin regretted that "racist attitudes have finally driven black men to abandon many of the old dreams we shared, dreams that were good; and to embark into this period of transition that so bewilders men, but in which we are *beginning to see our first real hope*."

Ironically, only by giving up that "dream of integration" could black thinkers move toward a philosophy entirely their own, developing a black consciousness as opposed to the "fragmented individualism" that denied their identity in the pursuit of white goals. Blackness was transformed into a sign of beauty and dignity, rather than internalized as negative images. This was a return to the celebration of sisterhood and brotherhood, based on self-determination, which was turning the black community from a ghetto of white-imposed separation into a communal space of unity.

Griffin began to discuss Black Power in his lectures to whites living in the North:

> Black thinkers — usually unknown to white America — began to structure and analyze the weakness of black America, and since their philosophical analyses conformed to their lived experience, much of it was immediately understood. This did not mean relinquishing the struggle for equal rights and justice, but perceiving it as a form of political desegregation rather than as a form of social integration with whites.
>
> Black Power rose to the surface at a time when this land faced a confrontation that appeared inevitably to lead to violence and to genocidal suppression of black people. Black Power rose, if men could only perceive it, as almost *a stroke of genius* that could avoid violence, that could turn the burning resentments and the energies they engendered, into healthful and constructive channels. Black Power, thus understood, implied not the advocacy of violence — as so many white believed — but the alternative to that kind of fruitless confrontation.

The most common criticism of Black Power was that it amounted to a form of reverse racism. This was a false analogy because black people had not lynched whites or burned down their churches or created obstacles at the voting booths. While racist attitudes, hate stares and epithets are capable of causing emotional pain, without the assumed power to cause bodily injury or to kill another human being with impunity, a racist attitude remains an attitude and nothing more. Many of the segregated areas of the Deep South during the 1960s were police states where racist Jim Crow statutes were codified as law. Any critique of the Black Liberation Movement must be viewed *not* as a matter of "progress" from the white perspective, but as a process of revolutionary consciousness-raising that lighted the cause of justice in a system that had cast a supremacist shadow over the democratic principals and religious ideals it claimed to espouse. Black Power could not change the culture's deeply entrenched institutions in the short term, but it did move the discourse toward a dialogue of equals.

Griffin's take on Malcolm X, written as a review of the 1975 book *The Death and Life of Malcolm X* by Peter Goldman, reveals not only the progressive depth in Griffin's awareness of racism after *Black Like Me* but also his openness to the spiritual character of Malcolm's quest (after his break with the Black Muslim hierarchy). Throughout this piece and all of the writings on racism, we can trace the spiritual references for Griffin's humanitarian views about justice denied to the *Other* in our culture.

The Spiritual Dimension

"Poulenc Behind the Mask" tells the story of the French classical composer and pianist, Francis Poulenc, with whom Griffin had a long correspondence during the 1950s. Poulenc was struggling with depression and his worthiness as a Catholic while working to finish the masterful opera, *Dialogue of the Carmelites*. After receiving a letter from cellist Zara Nelsova about Poulenc's deteriorating health, Griffin wrote the composer to offer the prayers of the Carmelites for the completion of his opera. Poulenc first responded to Griffin thinking that the "Third Order Carmelite" was a priest. Once that error was clarified, Poulenc beseeched Griffin for the prayers of the monks at Mount Carmel Seminary in Dallas. During this period Griffin was blind and at work on a second novel, *Nuni* (1954), as well as questioning his own faith in the same way as the composer. Griffin was certain he was *not* the person to help, but knew that the Carmelites, who had a deep interest in the opera about the early days of their Order, were the ideal choice.

Poulenc's correspondence and opera reveal a vulnerable soul behind the mask of the flamboyant public persona projected throughout his controversial life. Griffin compares the "bounder" he had met in France to the wounded artist in the letters. "And although I had met Poulenc in France—we had been neighbors in Tours in my school days and had encountered one another at concerts in Paris after World War II—he did not make this association. He poured out his agony in a way that I am sure he seldom did to anyone face-to-face. In his letters, he adjured me to silence until after his death. The correspondence reveals a Poulenc who does not coincide with his popular public image, or even with my own personal impression of him."

"Fraternal Dialogue" recounts Griffin's visit to the University of Peace in Huy, Belgium during the summer of 1964. No stranger to cloisters, he eagerly inhabited a cell in the Dominican Priory, constructed in 1834, which was "like the monasteries I used to know in France—truly poor and simple." Griffin's spirituality had been grounded in the monastic tradition, dating back to his retreat at the Abbey of Solesmes in France, evoked in his memoir *Scattered Shadows* (published posthumously in 2004).

Griffin was at the University of Peace to lecture to international students at the invitation of Dominique Pire, the architect of "Fraternal Dialogue" who had received the 1958 Nobel Peace Prize for his work on behalf of displaced persons after World War II. Griffin took his cameras and made a fine portrait of Father Pire, as well as scenes in the city and the countryside. During his stay, he learned of the murder of the three civil rights workers—James Chaney, Michael Schwerner and Andrew Goodman in Mississippi. (The full story can be read in Bruce Watson's great history, *Freedom Summer*, published in 2010.)

The essay's final words are: "The report says James Chaney (the Negro student) was severely beaten before being shot. Dehumanization of the racists. This is what I go back to, back to the rooms where I must look into the ravaged faces of

James Chaney's mother, or Clyde Kennard's mother and how many more mothers of martyrs before we learn to stop justifying our cheating?" No matter how far Griffin traveled, the news of white racism followed him—even into the cloister of the University of Peace in Belgium.

"The Little Brothers" tells the saga of the founder of this most austere order, Charles de Foucauld, who lived in absolute poverty alone in the desert where he was murdered in 1916. Father Foucauld's goal was to attract a small community of "little brothers" to the Sahara, but no one ventured there until *after* his death. "Ironically, they came into existence through the fact that Foucauld was like a great many men who seek to be the least known, but who tend to be so extraordinary that they instead become the best known." In a posthumously published book Griffin wrote something similar about the his friend, the Trappist monk and spiritual writer Thomas Merton, in *Follow the Ecstasy: The Hermitage Years of Thomas Merton* (1985). Griffin admired Foucauld greatly, considered joining the Order but could not because of blindness, and once gained permission to research a novel in the Sahara among the brothers that he did not follow up on. The second part of this essay is a portrait of two of the brothers in Detroit and the third part speaks of his spiritual mentor, Jacques Maritain, who joined the Little Brothers at their motherhouse in Toulouse, France, after the death of the French philosopher's wife Raïssa Maritain. Charles de Foucauld was beatified in 2005.

"The Terrain of Physical Pain" stands as Griffin's deepest personal essay, even while he speaks from a relatively objective viewpoint. He knew pain and suffering first hand, but since they are universal realities all humans know at some level he approached it as a multilayered intuition "beyond the realm of ideas." He draws upon the experiences of spiritual thinkers and artists, including his close friends, French poets Pierre Reverdy and Raïssa Maritain. From Reverdy we learn of the redemptive quality of suffering and from Maritain—her key insight about experiencing pain simultaneously on two levels which she described in her 1934 *Journal* as "this faculty to act at once on two planes—that of concrete experience, demanding and painful, and that of an abstract and liberating conception rooted in the same experience." According to Griffin, the sufferer begins "to perceive that self is less interesting," and "to learn the difference between what is merely average and what is normal." The average sufferer reacts as culture teaches, adopting the acceptable masks of stoicism and self-pity, whereas the humble sufferer plumbs unexpected levels of spirituality, extending compassion and love unconditionally to one's caregivers.

Lastly we have Griffin's "Final Reflections" about communication, justice and dying, from interviews with Thurston Smith and Studs Terkel, which include his last remarks about the core concepts he developed throughout his writing life.

John Howard Griffin died of a coronary on September 9, 1980, a few months after his 60th birthday. Yet during his relatively brief life, Griffin left an incredible legacy of ethical humanitarianism beyond *Black Like Me*, spiritual enlightenment without a hint of sanctimony, and artistic achievement in the areas of literature, photography and classical musicology.

Prison
of Culture

Part I

Lionel Trilling has remarked that culture is a prison unless we know the key that unlocks the door.

And it is a common anthropological truism that the "prisoners" of any given culture tend to regard those of almost any other culture, no matter how authentic that culture, as merely underdeveloped versions of their own imprisoning culture.

Racist attitudes begin benignly enough from this basic concept of the other as intrinsically Other. Once one views others as "different," the stereotype develops.

—John Howard Griffin, "The Intrinsic *Other*" (1966)

Privacy of Conscience

After the publication of *Black Like Me*, everyone was after me to explain my motive for doing such a thing. In the first place, it was nobody's damned business what my motives were. There is no more respect for the privacy of conscience. I tell them simply, I don't want my children becoming racists. And that's a good enough answer, even though it's not the real answer. I don't want any children to grow up to be nasty little klansmen with distorted views of what fellow human beings are. But the very idea of anyone probing into the privacy of another man's conscience is almost the greatest obscenity.

I think we have to struggle to grant every man the maximum amount of freedom and so I loathe every kind of totalitarianism. I don't care where it comes from, I loathe anything that impugns a man's right to fulfill himself. And certainly totalitarianism implies the suppression of fellow human beings in one way or the other. We have to work to assure every man the maximum right to function as fully and freely as possible. There is no such thing as an inherent right to impugn someone else's rights; and it is an utter distortion to claim the freedom to deny someone else's freedom. We must see that all men truly have equal rights and then just leave everybody alone. This trying to gobble everyone up, to make him conform to our individual or group prejudices, our religious or philosophical convictions—and seeking to suppress him if he doesn't—is the deepest cultural neurosis I know.

I utterly refuse to judge a man's motives because I don't think you can know a man's motives. I think this is a frightful, obscene thing to do. I think it is also highly dubious. Any man— the moment he impugns my rights or your rights—must be battled, because he is involved in a terrible thing; he is involved in the destruction of the common good.

These things come from far deeper. I think the most vicious racists I have encountered have a disease. There is nobody for whom I feel a deeper pity than these distorted human beings.

And I have studied them for over twenty-five years without having the slightest certainty that I know one bit more about their motives now than I did then.

What I do know is the culturation that they have gone through, the formation: they are imprisoned in these cultural, learned behavior patterns and are frightfully handicapped by them. How can you set up norms for either discovering or interpreting the motives of people with a great complex set of neuroses? I think the very act, at least by a layman, is an essentially degrading thing. It degrades the person who is doing it rather than the person to whom it is done.

We have read a great many postmortem analyses, we have read all these analyses of Hitler, but I don't think we know enough. We are only now discovering the effects of biochemistry on the nervous system. How can you know these things, particularly when you are doing it on the basis of letters, or on the basis of conversations that people have had? How can you know that some killer didn't have high blood sugar on the day that caused him to detach from conscious awareness?

I think it is a mistake to examine your motives too closely. The most damaging aphorism in history is the aphorism: "Know Thyself." The quicker you can lose interest in yourself, the better you can function as a human being. I have a lot of young people write me, doing wonderful things, but worried to death about the truth of their motives. I discourage them from this kind of examination. Because if we act only from the purest, most balanced, most healthy motives, we would come to a screeching standstill. What do we do from pure motives? It is a kind of self-pride even to discover those things and it seems to me the quicker you get rid of self-consciousness the better you can function. Who cares? What a monstrous kind of pride this is. You can examine yourself to a halt in all, until you are afraid to do anything. And I don't think it is interesting what one's motives are once the act is done.

The main theme of the work about racism centers on this prison of cultural formation that almost always leads a man of one culture to believe that he is intrinsically different from men of other cultures. And profoundly different: different in his aspirations, needs, responses to stimuli. This is one of the most difficult problems involved in racism. We tend to think that the victim group somehow likes it that way; that its members respond to frustration, for example, in a manner totally different from us. And along with this, goes that other tendency to view members of all other cultures as merely underdeveloped versions of ourselves. We get the ugly American, then; and the missionary mentality that wants always to bring the other cultures up to "our level."

I helped prepare a program for French National Television about this a couple of years ago. We demonstrated that when racism begins, the first thing that goes out the window is respect for due process of law. We documented it with cases of black people in the South being involved in block round-ups, not informed of their rights, and denied them if they happened to know these rights. When the pattern is established, then it spreads to any non-member of a victim group who happens *not* to be a racist. When we were certain all of France was outraged, we did the last twenty minutes in France, showing exactly the same patterns held with the Arab population in Paris. They were picked up, subjected to third degree methods, denied due process.

These are the basic patterns that can lead men from an apparently benign form of racism to the most vicious forms. They know how quickly the one can pave the way for the other, how quickly the little *yeses* can lead to the great and terrible *yeses* that have scarred the lives of so many victims of racism. And these basic patterns hold. Any black person gets them to the point of nausea.

For example, in lecturing throughout this land, going rapidly from one city to another, I speak to crowds of sincere and concerned people. I will be warmly received. Afterward, in almost every community, someone of importance will come to me, shake my hand and say how good it is to hear these great principles clarified. But then, in virtually every instance, he will add: "But, of course, we have a different situation here." One gets the uneasy impression that we are becoming a nation of exceptions to the very principles that we applaud and think we espouse.

The same holds true in Europe. When I lectured in Belgium on the problem of racism, I was enthusiastically received. After one lecture, a doctor came to me with tears in his yes and grasped my hand, explaining that he had been a missionary in Africa for fifteen years.

"What a marvelous speech," he said. "But of course our situation in the Congo is different. American blacks are so much more evolved than our poor Congolese. American blacks should have all their rights. It is going to take generations before our Congolese are ready for their rights."

How familiar it sounded. There were five Congolese in the audience, and I could not resist introducing them to the doctor. One had a licentiate in International Law, another was preparing his licentiate; two others had Ph.D.'s; and the fifth was a physician. The Belgian doctor was charmed by them, but never got the point.

Later, I could not keep quiet and told him: "Doctor, you have met one hundred percent of my Congolese audience tonight. Each of those men was born in the bush. Just how *un*evolved can a people get?"

Since James Baldwin hurled the challenge at "white" Christianity to put up or shut up, we have seen some reevaluation and even some important changes, but these are far from being sufficiently widespread as yet to nullify the deep scandal of segregation. Black people often have contempt for what they call "the white man's God."

We have driven blacks to this stance and thereby alienated men in the deepest and most damaging way — a way that damages not only the victim group but the total community. A good deal of the contempt of the young for my generation's values springs directly from this, and we should thank God our failures appear so disgusting to them.

I heard it put very accurately in a session with a group of Chicago slum priests. Father Fichter, a noted sociologist at Yale, remarked: "We have consistently failed to do what we know is right out of a fear of what might hypothetically happen." I have never heard it said better. Almost the first reaction of churchmen is: "Yes, but if we do such and such, it might lead to an even worse condition." Seldom do I hear churchmen say that such and such is either morally right or wrong, or even base their judgments on the very principles they profess.

If I had known how it would develop, I would have written *Black Like Me* more completely. I thought, and my publishers agreed, that this would be an obscure work, of interest primarily to sociologists. I therefore limited the experiment to the Deep South, and I also did not include a number of experiences. I failed, for example, to write much about religious institutions. I have been criticized for this, and it is a most valid criticism. I did not write about it for two reasons.

First, I was so deeply shocked to be driven away from churches which would have welcomed me any time as a white man that I did not know how to handle this. I feared I might be committing an injustice to write about it without proper time to think about it. Second, in my naiveté, I was certain that as soon as these conditions were made known to the Church leadership, the matter would be corrected. Well, I made them known and was given only the most blatant kinds of rationalizations to justify them by the very leadership I had thought would bring corrective measures. When I saw that nothing was going to be done, that the official Church was not going to rock any boats, I published a piece about my own confusion after being driven from the "house of God" when outside I heard the voices from within singing hymns to Jesus.

Perhaps my major fascination as a novelist is centered around man's pressures to become part of the crowd, part of the scene, part of the monolith. I am tremendously preoccupied with the problems of loners, or men who struggle to go it alone. To go with the crowd makes a man seek the average instead of what is truly his own normalcy, his own truth. Men do this and end up being all alike—one mediocrity is like another—and they realize too late. All the pressures of society tend to conformity, to the crowd, to the monolith that eventually tries to destroy the one who is different, the one who has tried to be true to his vision. The merely average hates true normalcy, as though it were hating the reminder of a dream long lost.

In Nazi Germany it ended up killing everything that differed from the average, everything that did not fit the monolith. It is an historic problem. Pascal knew it when he said we must speak like the crowd but hold our own thoughts secret. Sometimes men have to follow that sorry advice because society will kill them. But if they follow it long enough, they end up having no "true" thoughts to keep secret.

Again, it is the problem of the intrinsic *Other*. It is a problem that grows rapidly in this land where too many men are coming to the conclusion that perhaps we had better put the dissenters in jail; put those who think differently out of the way; and destroy them for the very freedom we loudly claim for the crowd.

—1966

The Intrinsic *Other*

Lionel Trilling has remarked that culture is a prison unless we know the key that unlocks the door.

And it is a common anthropological truism that the "prisoners" of any given culture tend to regard those of almost any other culture, no matter how authentic that culture, as merely underdeveloped versions of their own imprisoning culture.

The language that men use constantly reveals this attitude. We then hear of: "The immoral French. The godless Russians. The snobbish English. The shifty Orientals. The grasping Jew. The savage Negro. And the ugly American."

Even when we may be totally unaware that we possess such attitudes of racial or ethnic superiority, our language expresses these judgments in a glaringly clear manner. "Some of my best friends are Jews," we say. Or, "Personally, I am very fond of Negroes, but I would not want to live next door to one."

One of characteristics of our expression of such attitudes is that they are often perfectly natural to the speaker and unnatural to the hearer. They reveal in the speaker the falsity of viewing others as *intrinsically other*, intrinsically different as men. This intrinsic difference always implies some degree of inferiority.

Racist attitudes begin benignly enough from this basic concept of the other as intrinsically *Other*. Once one views others as "different," the stereotype develops.

Implicit in this process is a consent to racism. Edmund Burke gave us the touchstone of this error when he said: "I know of no way of drawing up an indictment against a whole people."

Racism begins when we draw up an indictment against a whole people merely by considering them as a whole underdeveloped versions of ourselves, by perpetuating the blindness of the stereotype.

The Nazis drew up an indictment against a whole people, the world Jewish community. And once the indictment was drawn, and far more importantly, once mankind consented to the indictment and did not cry *No!*—the rest followed: the dehumanization of the total community, Jewish and Nazi.

In America and Africa, we have drawn up an indictment against whole peoples, the dark-skinned peoples. This has led to the dehumanization of all men, white and black. And once the error is accepted, then other victim groups are engulfed. The Klans of America are not only anti-Negro, but anti-Jewish, anti-Catholic, anti-*Other*.

Let me repeat that this is insidious, because it is often done in good faith, is often accomplished with an illusion of benevolence. It leads to master delusion. The delusion lies in the fact that no matter how well we think we know the *Other*, we still judge from within the imprisoning framework of our own limited cultural criteria, we speak within the cliché of the stereotype.

I have known missionaries, splendidly cultivated men, who have spent years in other cultures without ever penetrating the other culture, who go on judging everything by the limited criteria of the educated European or American. In my own life, this error was once thrown in my face.

I was living on a Pacific island doing language studies. I considered, with great affection, my subjects to be "primitives" or "aboriginals" and even "unevolved people." There was no question but that theirs was an "inferior" and mine a "superior" culture. They were *Other*.

After many months on the island, however, whenever I went from one village to another through the jungles, I still had to have a five-year-old lad guide me. If I were lost, I would not have known how to survive, what to eat in the jungles. It became obvious to me that within the context of that culture, I was clearly inferior—an adult man who could not have survived without the guidance of a child. And from the point of view of the local inhabitants—a valid point of view—I was *Other*, inferior, and they were superior.

But such perceptions are difficult because our culture forms us in attitudes at the emotional level very early in our lives. These learned behavior patterns are so profoundly ingrained in us that we tend to call them human nature, which they are not at all. But nevertheless, even when we are intellectually liberated from our prejudices, we often remain emotionally imprisoned by them.

My own experience, living as a Negro in the South, overwhelmingly demonstrated this. Almost the deepest shock I had came the first night that I went out into the New Orleans night as a Negro. I went to a hotel in the ghetto and took the best available room—a tawdry, miserable little cubbyhole. I sat on the bed and glanced at myself in the mirror on the wall. For the first time I was alone as a Negro in the Negro community. That glance in the mirror brought a sickening shock that I tried not to admit, not to recognize, but I could not avoid it.

It was the shock of seeing my black face in the mirror and of feeling an involuntary movement of antipathy for that face, because it was pigmented. I realized then that although intellectually I had liberated myself from the prejudices which our Southern culture inculcates in us, these prejudices were so profoundly indredged in me that at the emotional level I was in no way liberated. I was filled with despair.

Here I had come all this way, had myself transformed chemically into a black man, because of my profound intellectual convictions about racism and prejudice, only to find that my own prejudices, at the emotional level, were hopelessly ingrained in me.

However, within five days, that involuntary movement of antipathy was completely dissipated, because within five days I was living in the homes of Negro families and experiencing emotionally what intellectually I had long known—that the *Other* was not other at all.

Within the context of home and family life we faced exactly the same problems in the homes of Negroes as those faced in all homes of all men: the universal problems of loving, of suffering, of bringing children to the light, of fulfilling human aspirations, of dying.

Therefore, the wounds that I had carried thirty-nine years of my life were healed within five days through the emotional experience of perceiving that the *Other* is not other at all, that the *Other* is me, that at the profound human levels, all men are united; and that the seeming differences are superficial. The illusion of the *Other*, of these superficial differences, is deeply imbedded through this inculcated stereotype we make of the *Other*, which falsifies man's view of man.

The French thinker Jean Lacroix has said that before one can truly dialogue in depth, one must open oneself to the *Other*. I think this is not enough. I believe that before we can truly dialogue in depth, we must first perceive that there is no *Other*, that the *Other* is oneself in all essentials, and that the I-and-Thou concept of philosopher Martin Buber must finally dissolve itself into the *We* concept.

It seems to me that this and this alone is the key that can unlock the prison of culture. It is also the key that will neutralize the poisons of the stereotype that allow men to go on benevolently justifying their abuses against other men.

—1965

Profile of A Racist

I have encountered two types of racists.

The one who has no respect for one whom Jean Lacroix calls the *Other*—in other words, for any form of human life other than his own. This type of racist allows his lack of respect to form the permissive basis for cruelty, sadism, violence and murder. He feels he has the right to indulge those subhuman lusts. He even feels he has the duty to indulge them (for the good of society). He is almost always a fanatic, since fanaticism breeds fanaticism, and he ties himself into a religion in the most outspoken way.

The other kind of racist abhors, or claims to, the orgiastic cruelties, but has no respect for life, for the living and breathing and suffering of the *Other*. He denounces the lynching, but clings hard to the very ideology that makes lynching permissive and even inevitable. He weaves the lynch rope that he himself would not use.

He is the gentleman who speaks fine words: "We have to take these things slowly. You can't legislate morality. It may take a few more generations. You can't cram justice down people's throats."

His fine words cloak the same old racist cadaver. He asks that we respect "necessary evil" for some time to come. He suggests that it is a mark of profound disrespect to ask men to render justice if they are deeply prejudiced.

—1965

On *Killers of the Dream*

Lillian Smith, as the whole world surely knows, is a Southern Lady. Twelve years ago with prophetic vision, she wrote *Killers of the Dream* (1950), a book about the South and segregation. In it she showed that those who embraced the strangely shallow dream of white supremacy were killers of the greater American dream of a society based on freedom, equality and justice.

Now the book has been updated and published again in 1962. It has no warmed-over-hash character, largely because of the superb vitality and validity of the original. Also because it is a highly original work of art—distilled, concentrated, terrible, and beautiful. If one sets out to underline the most significant or telling passages, one must underline most of the sentences in the book.

Lillian Smith was born and reared in the South, a member of a cultivated and respected family. She learned, as did all children of good families, the lessons of that southern culture.

> The mother who taught me what I know of tenderness and love and compassion taught me also the bleak rituals of keeping Negroes in their 'place.' The father who rebuked me for an air of superiority toward schoolmates from the mill and rounded out his rebuke by gravely reminding me that 'all men are brothers,' trained me in the steel-rigid decorums I must demand of every colored male. They who so gravely taught me to split my body from my mind and both from my 'soul,' taught me also to split my conscience from my acts and Christianity from southern tradition.

The southern girls learned other things—a puritanical crushed-violet concept of sex, kindness to the Negro, the superiority of whiteness. They learned that Christ appointed the southern white to care for the well-being of the southern Negro, and that segregation was the proper and Christian way to insure the happiness of *both* races. They learned that it was unkind to encourage the Negro beyond the barriers erected for his own good.

They learned that "old mammy" was not worthy of the passionate love they felt for her. "I learned the bitterest thing a child can learn: that the human relations I valued most were held cheap by the world I lived in," writes Smith.

Most important of all, they learned that a Southern White Woman is sacred — a sacred reality who must be protected from the lion that raged beneath the thin layer of domestication nurtured in the *black* by the *white*. Open the door to the Negro's cage and the lion would bound out to rape the white sacredness, to despoil it and outrage heaven . . . and also create a servant problem.

The southern white woman had her flowers, her kitchen, her illusion of sacredness. And there was a certain beauty in all of this if she swallowed her frustrations at being cheated by the husband who had chivalrously guarded her sacredness by lavishing his brute masculinity on Negro women and saving only the gentle leftovers for his wife.

Many intelligent southerners felt the contradictions of such a culture. "I learned to believe in freedom, to glow when the word *democracy* was used, and to practice slavery from morning to night." How did one live in such a delusion? ". . . by closing door after door until one's mind and heart and conscience were blocked off from each other and from reality."

For Lillian Smith these doors could not remain forever closed. Intelligence could not forever be denied. Certainly, it was the same for others. Why then did so few question the "system," speak out and call it the delusion it was? Because the great teacher, the supreme Authority, Tradition, taught that nothing was more odious than the radical. ". . . you accepted it all uncritically. You insisted on others accepting it also. You dreaded the deviationist, you were in horror lest your children be other than orthodox southerners." And there was danger. The demagogues used the race question to incite sexual fears, wore down the whites' belief in human decency until the people would commit violence against "any individual or group . . .

different from them, convinced that anyone 'different' was their mortal enemy."

But the thing had started for Lillian Smith; she began to see, to think, to ponder. She began to understand "that the warped, distorted frame we put around every Negro child from birth is around every white child also . . . And I knew that what cruelly shapes and cripples the personality of one is cruelly shaping and crippling the personality of the other."

She cut through the layers of falsity and arrived at the inevitable conclusion—the southern white woman was not the *only* a sacred reality. Every human creature was a *res sacra*. And she saw here the key to it: the moment the racist or anyone else for a second treated any person, in any condition, as less than a sacred reality, there were no limits to the ultimate effects of evil.

Once she saw this, she saw the full terror of it, and its ramifications in world politics. She rightly foresaw that the resonances of this "local" even could eventually destroy the whole country by turning the world away from us toward the Communist ideology.

She thought "our people can change quickly if given convincing reasons," and wrote this semi-autobiographical work that "recreates the southern experience." In it she creates understanding at the level of lived experience; the reader sees, smells, feels all the elements that go into the formation of the southerner, and feels profound sympathy.

Lillian Smith makes poignant the tremendous forces that have entrapped southern whites. She asks: "Are we—the nation that first embarked on the high adventure of making a world fit for human beings to live in—about to destroy ourselves because we have killed our dream?"

And she answers: "Time has run out: we must right now adjust ourselves to the speed and quality of world events, world moods, world psychology or face probable extinction as a free nation."

She slashes to the core of falsity and warns that we have no more time for this mass self-indulgence even though "our demagogues at home and in Congress are still wailing about mixing and mongrelizing . . . and 'agitators'; and still giving communism credit for every brave, intelligent, decent act done by a southerner." And all of this is written with such vehemence that is the overflow of her vast compassion.

Surely, *Killers of the Dream*, from the pen of a remarkably cultivated and communicative intellect, is the master contribution to our understanding of the most gangrenous problem of our time.

—1962

Requiem For A Martyr

Clyde Kennard was one of the great men of our times. He is known by very few, and yet no less a person than Jacques Maritain, the renowned French philosopher, described him this way: "I have no doubt that Clyde Kennard's life and martyrdom are among the most significant events of our age."

Kennard was born in Mississippi and served ten years as a paratrooper for his country in Germany and in Korea. He saved his money, and when he returned home he bought some land in Mississippi that he turned over to his mother and stepfather. Kennard then moved away to attend the University of Chicago, where he was a brilliant student.

But after three years his stepfather died and Clyde had to return home to take over the farm and care for his mother, Mrs. Leona Smith. He made a successful business of the farm and paid his taxes. Then he applied to what was then Mississippi Southern College, because he wanted to complete his undergraduate degree. The college was twelve miles away from home, a school supported completely by state tax funds. While no black man had ever attended the local college, the school's administration could find no way to keep him out. His scholastic and military service records were distinguished. However, by the kind of cruel control that could be made to appear coincidental, Clyde was arrested on a reckless driving charge the very day he registered at the college. He was taken to the station in a police car while a second officer drove Clyde's car.

When this second officer walked into the station, he carried a sack of five bottles of whiskey, which he claimed he had found in Kennard's car. Clyde never drank alcohol, but he was charged with illegal possession of whiskey. However, when the police realized that it would require a felony charge to keep Kennard out of the college, they arranged for more serious trumped-up charges. He was accused by a nineteen-year-old mentally retarded Negro, who had been arrested three days earlier for selling stolen chicken feed. The young man confessed, but was manipulated into claiming he had sold twenty-five dollars worth of that chicken feed to Kennard, saying Clyde had purchased it knowing that it had been stolen.

In one of the most farcical trials and travesties of justice ever witnessed, the young man was found guilty of having stolen the feed and was given a suspended sentence. Clyde was found guilty of having bought it and was given seven years of hard labor. He was put in prison and at first was treated well. But soon he developed intestinal cancer and was put in a hospital in Jackson. It happened that this was at the same time that James Meredith made his first tentative move to enter the University of Mississippi. The two men had no connection whatsoever—except that they were black men in the South— but through a strange kind of vengeance, Clyde was taken out of the hospital and put on the hardest work gang at the penitentiary.

Though his cancer developed rapidly, this extraordinary man spent his Sundays writing letters for inmates who could not read or write, and began to set up classes to teach them reading and writing. But when he became too ill, he wrote his sister, a registered nurse in Chicago, that he was beginning to hemorrhage. She reached the doctor in Jackson who immediately ordered Clyde back into the hospital. The doctor's prognosis was that he had less than a twenty percent chance of surviving, under even optimum conditions. But the warden refused to let Clyde return to the hospital.

As Clyde became very weak, he began to realize that the state officials were deliberately allowing him to die. He would be carried out in the mornings, and he would work until he would collapse, and then he would be carried back. And when he began to collapse before noon each day, they would carry him back to his bed. If he was unable to get up and walk to the mess hall, which was the case, he would go without food because they did not allow food to be brought to him.

Finally, a group of us—Dr. Martin Luther King, Jr., Dick Gregory, and others—discussed this, and we began to put pressure on Governor Ross Barnett. We virtually said that if Clyde Kennard died in prison it would be murder. Almost immediately, he was released.

We found out the last events of his imprisonment from his family. His mother and sister had gone to see him and bring him food. They found him bleeding badly, starving, and weighing less than one 100 pounds. The next morning when the prisoners came to carry him out, he said they would have to leave him on the ground at the work site, because he could not work. His fellow prisoners saw it was useless to carry him out so they called a guard and Clyde was taken by car to the prison doctor.

The guard's only words to him were: "Damn you, if you mess up this car, I'll kick you out." He was left in the doctor's waiting room. After a few steps, Clyde's legs gave way, and this enormously gifted man, an American soldier and scholar, who had been framed by a racist System, ended up crawling on his belly to the examination room. And there the doctor said: "We know what's happened. You can't pull this kind of thing here. I know that smart-aleck sister of yours brought you some food and she probably put some pills in it that made you so sick you wouldn't have to go on the work gang."

Clyde had the presence of mind to ask that the doctor examine him to see if this were possible. The doctor did, and he saw that Clyde was very close to death. He told the warden who notified the Governor's office. The Governor immediately gave an indefinite pardon, so that the state of Mississippi would not have this prisoner's dead body on their hands.

He was brought to Chicago for an eight-hour operation and briefly there was hope for temporary recovery. I went to visit him at his request. The doctor said Clyde had given up hope, however, and that he could not keep him alive if he did not have the will to live. This did not sound like Clyde, but the doctor said that someone who had visited told him that vandals had moved onto his farm at night and burned down some of the buildings. This seemed to have been the final blow.

The post-operative tests showed that it was too late and that Clyde would be dead within a matter of weeks. I went in to see him. He lay with a sheet pulled up over his face so no one could see the grimace of pain.

When I spoke, he revealed his face, graciously thanking me for visiting him. Curiously, he was the one who consoled me, as he had consoled other visitors.

And then he said something that almost killed me: "Mr. Griffin, I'd be glad it happened if only it would show this country where racism finally leads. But people are not going to know it, are they?"

"They'll know it, because I will speak of it in every lecture."

Then this man who had suffered such agony for three years said: "Be sure to tell them that what happened to me isn't as bad as what has happened to that guard, because this system has turned him into a beast, and it will turn his children into beasts." This great man died with this kind of magnanimity, sending out this kind of message.

After he died, I asked his mother, Mrs. Leona Smith, "How can we stand it? This isn't America. This is Dachau and Auschwitz. This was a man who had great things to contribute, and because he wanted to finish his education in an area where he had every right, where his tax dollars supported the school, he was thrown to the mad dogs and ended up a martyr." She made no reply but the deepest grief I have ever witnessed was etched on her face.

I thought about what was said at the end of the Nuremberg trials when the judge asked: "How did we come to this appalling mistake?"

The prosecuting attorney answered: "You opened the door the first time you knowingly condemned an innocent man."

But whenever we defraud men of rights, which are inherent in their being men and citizens, we are knowingly condemning innocent men; we are doing what Burke said was logically and ethically impossible: We are drawing up an indictment against a whole people.

—1963

Racist Sins of Christians

In 1963, two groups of American citizens are hurtling toward one another in a conflict that can result in an urban civil war. I have toured the entire country—with an additional two survey trips through the Deep South—and I am convinced that a Negro-white clash is inevitable. While the North and South have wasted time bickering about which is worse, Negroes, particularly young Negroes, have lost their illusions about "good whites." They have seen us equivocate endlessly and finally grow silent in times of crisis, when issues were clear and words of protest or sanity would have sounded with clarion clarity.

Racism—discrimination based on skin color—has grown strong, hard, and bitter throughout the length and breadth of America. Racists who claim to be anti-Communists do Communism's work magnificently well by showing the world our racist abuses and thereby turning the world from us in disgust.

The recent murder of Medgar Evers in Jackson, Mississippi, the hideous martyrdom of Clyde Kennard, and the truthful revelations of James Baldwin and Martin Luther King, Jr. have shocked Americans. We are now a deeply concerned people, but we are not well informed.

White Americans and Negro Americans, communicating at only the most superficial level, tend to see the same event in entirely different lights. Whites view the growing Negro militancy with fear.

Negroes view it as the only solution, because they can see little hope that whites will voluntarily grant them their rights— and they can no longer live without these rights. Negroes grow more determined as they grow more disillusioned by the cheating, continued harassment, the obstructionism that is openly practiced all over American against any move to exercise their civil rights.

Negroes are well-informed, through their own news media, of the constant racist depredations. Since newspapers seldom carry controversial material, the non-Negro public is only vaguely informed. I have seen the same brutality in New York City that I have seen in Mississippi. I have seen the same lack of communication between Negro and white citizens in Cleveland, Detroit, Los Angeles, Rochester, and Buffalo that I have seen in Alabama.

Uninformed, the national conscience cannot manifest itself. We remain two groups of citizens with two different sets of information who do not trust one another and who cannot discuss our problems at a sufficiently profound depth.

My information about and attitude toward the crisis today are deeply influenced by an experience three years ago when I had a dermatologist darken my skin, and I lived as a Negro in the Deep South. Behind the sociological experiment there lay the profound conviction that our most corrosive problem was *not* a racial problem but *a problem of racism*—and that unless this problem of racism were understood, it could destroy us.

In my teens, as a medical student in France, I had seen the extremes to which racism could lead when I helped smuggle German and Austrian Jews from the Nazi "final solution." I had seen men and women of great quality destroyed because they were born of Jewish parents.

Later, in America, I had made studies of crisis community patterns in areas where racial prejudice subverted justice. These studies showed appalling parallels to the growth of anti-Semitism I had witnessed in Europe. Mental attitudes were similar. In Germany particularly, a man was condemned, not by his qualities as a human being, but because he was Jewish. In America, skin pigmentation was enough to condemn a man to second-class citizenship.

The folly of racism which discriminated against a man because of the color of his skin was dramatically illustrated to me during ten years when I was blinded by a war injury. The blind learn to judge an individual by his qualities as a human being. To the sightless we are all human individuals, more or less good, more or less cultivated, more or less intelligent. Our physical attractiveness, lightness or darkness of skin color do not enter the picture.

When I was blind, it seemed a grotesque abuse of the gift of sight to prevent any man from fulfilling his human potential merely because his skin was dark. Yet we were doing this in America and bringing up our children to follow in our footsteps, despite the fact that scientists were every day denouncing concepts of racial inferiority or superiority.

Listening one evening to the Beethoven *Opus 132 Quartet*, one of the sublimest utterances in all music, I realized that if Beethoven had lived in the South today, he would be considered a Negro, a second-class human. I, as a white man in the South, could not sit down at a restaurant table with St. Martin of Porres or St. Benedict the Moor, though I could eat there with the most derelict white person.

I decided that the only way to demonstrate what racism does to a human being was to become a Negro and experience it from the side that no white man can really know. I had a deep concern for the Negro as a victim of racism, but I had an equally deep concern for the white who, whether he realized it or not, was also a victim of racism. Obviously, the situation that warps and handicaps the Negro children—perhaps even more terribly—warps and handicaps white children.

On a chilly November 1959 night in New Orleans, after ten days of treatments by a dermatologist, I was ready to enter the world as a Negro. I was evenly dark from head to foot, and I had shaved my head. Otherwise, I was the same. I retained my name, my credentials, my speech pattern.

I decided that if I were questioned, I would answer truthfully. In the next six weeks, no white man asked my name; no one questioned my identity as a Negro.

But if I remained essentially the same man, everything about my life was drastically altered. Doors of dignity and self-respect that had been opened to me as a white man were closed to me as a Negro.

The full impact of it hit me that first night when I was directed to the best hotel accommodations for Negroes. It was a wretched little place in the ghetto. I asked for the best room and paid in advance. The proprietor led me up rickety stairs to the second floor. My "best room" was a cubicle scarcely larger than a double bed. It had no windows. I locked the door and began to undress. Noise of talk, laughter, and juke box jazz from a nearby tavern drifted through the thin clapboard walls.

I turned out the light and crawled into bed. A dog yowled somewhere in the distance. I lay awake in the oppressive closeness and felt desolation spread through me. For the first time, a statement came form my lips that I have heard Negroes utter countless times since: "It doesn't make any sense."

What sense did it make?

Here I was, the same John Howard Griffin who had often been an honored guest in New Orleans. I had been there on concert tours with the French pianist Robert Casadesus. I had been received in the finest homes, the finest hotels, the finest restaurants. I was that same man, with the same characteristics, even the same wallet.

But because my skin was black, all of those doors were closed. No amount of money could buy better accommodations. I lay in a wretched hole, because I was a Negro. I realized that if my pigmentation were permanently dark, my wife and children would have these same wretched accommodations and I would have to see them deprived.

In the next few days, I looked for jobs. I answered some want ads by telephone. My credentials often elicited interest, and I was virtually assured of the job, until I appeared for the interview. Then, when they saw I was a Negro, I was courteously turned away. There was no question that I could have earned a decent living as a white man.

As a Negro, the best jobs I held were shining shoes and unloading trucks. Only in the professions or after a long period of working oneself up could a Negro make a decent living. So I worked hard for my three or four dollars a day. In this economic bracket, my diet was reduced to rice and beans. This was delicious and cheap, but after a week of eating little else, my mind tended to pray, "Give us this day our daily beans...." Of course, many whites are poor and subsist on inadequate diets. But the important difference is that they are *not* kept poor because of their skin color.

And yet, New Orleans was a disarmingly courteous city. Individual whites treated me with great courtesy. But all of the courtesies in the world do not long mask the one massive discourtesy of segregation that inexorably banishes the Negro to humanity's junk heap. This involves being the victim of what Negroes call the "System"—this System is a complex of customs and traditions so deeply ingrained in the southern white that they have all the force of law, plus actual Jim Crow ordinances. Though it may vary in its details from locality to locality, the System says that American Negroes are indeed citizens and, as such, should pay taxes and defend their country from its enemies but that they should *not* vote or have equal protection under the law.

The System also says that they will not receive equality in educational or employment opportunities and that they should *not* have the use of public parks and beaches (even though their tax dollars help maintain these) or of public eating places, hotels, libraries, concert halls, and hospitals. The System contrives, in a thousand subtle ways, to defraud them of constitutional rights, and to deprive them of developing their full potential, thereby depriving America of their full contribution as citizens.

The System plunges a whole group of citizens in to intimate misery. As a Negro, I soon felt this misery. It consisted in facing daily the mountain of rebuffs that struck me from the very core of the System. Those rebuffs are unknown to the white man.

As a white, I had always been free to walk into a nearby door whenever hunger, thirst, or restroom needs made themselves felt. As a Negro, I quickly learned what it meant not to be free to walk through such doors. It can be a humiliating frustration to need restroom facilities and to discover that you must go halfway across town to find a place that will accommodate men of your color. Getting a drink of water was no longer simple. It meant searching, asking questions, locating places.

I began to see WHITE ONLY signs in a new way—as a cruel rebuff to nature and humanity. This was not a matter of mere inconvenience. It goes far deeper. Life turns somber when a man is never for a moment free from this grinding concern over the purely animal aspects of existence. The System kept my mind crammed down into my viscera, and I grew to hate the senseless degradation of it. All Negroes do.

Because of the System, daily life seldom rises above a mood of smoldering resentment over such indignities. The fact that Negroes often hide this resentment in order to survive does not mean they become inured to it. This reality is the obsession at all levels of society in the Negro community.

And like all Negroes, I soon found myself imprisoned in the stereotype. And yet I never encountered a Negro who fitted this stereotype which white men have contrived in order to justify racist injustice and to salve their consciences.

My soul shriveled to sit with a group of sensitive human beings, and listen to what the radio told us of our plight. A white woman with a marvelously patronizing voice spoke of our "earning" our rights to full citizenship—this in a country where every American is born with those rights and where Negroes have fought in wars to defend them for all.

One night, we sat in the ghetto squalor and heard a politician warn the public that any move toward racial justice that might give us the hope of human dignity was "playing into the Communists' hands." And he concluded that the System was "for the Negro's own good."

We stared at our dark hands and wondered if he had any idea what a massive crime he was committing. The deepest irony for us was to see white racists act always under the guise of patriotism and Christianity.

Many white men came to the shoe shine stand where I worked with Sterling Williams on a skid row street in New Orleans. Some wanted us to help them find guilty pleasures— girls, gambling, obscene photographs. We learned to spot them, for they treated us with a conniving friendliness and "equality." I mentioned this to Sterling, an elderly Negro veteran who had lost a leg in World War I.

"Oh, yes," he remarked astutely. "The whites are much more democratic in their sinning than in their worship."

I did not immediately realize the profound scandal

involved in his words, and certainly I did not connect it with the Catholic Church. What struck me was that the racist who spoke so often of the lower morals of Negroes appeared to live on a much lower moral level than I found among Negroes. The white man's concern for "racial purity" did not extend to the colored race, as any Negro soon learns.

That afternoon, as we prepared to quit work, I asked Sterling where I could find the nearest Catholic church.

"I guess the closest *colored* Catholic church would be way over on Dryades Street," he said.

"There's no such thing as a *colored* Catholic church," I replied quickly.

He looked up in astonishment. "You don't really believe that, do you?"

I assured him I did. "I know some churches practice segregation," I said, "but the Archbishop right here in New Orleans declared segregation a grave mortal sin."

"You're black now, John," my companion said in a gentle voice. "And this is the South. You're going to find that a lot of white Catholics look on you as a nigger first and a Catholic second, no matter what the Archbishop says. And a nigger Catholic has got to stay in his place, just like any other nigger."

I left the shoe shine stand, deciding to test the truth of Sterling's statements. Making my way on foot to the other side of the ghetto, I reached Dryades Street, mounted the steps of St. John the Baptist Catholic Church and opened one of the heavy doors. Street noises were muffled with its closing. Soft light filtered through magnificent stained glass windows in this oldest of New Orleans' churches—once a church for Catholics, now a church for Negro Catholics.

I sat in a pew, dwarfed in the vast structure, and leaned forward with my head against the bench in front. Glancing down a my hands, I saw each black wrinkle, each dark pore. This blackness condemned me out in the world, but the blessed illusion of sanctuary within the Church was so intense that I could not believe it condemned me here. I was home. I belonged here as much as any man. I felt superbly safe from that incessant threat of humiliation which daily accompanies the Negro.

I knew the Church's teaching allowed for no racial distinction between members of the human family. It regarded man as a *res sacra*, a sacred reality. God created all men with equal rights and equal dignity. The color of skin did not matter. What mattered was the quality of soul.

I recalled a statement made by Father J. Stanley Murphy: "Whenever any man permits himself to regard any other man, in any condition, as anything less than a *res sacra*, then the potentiality for evil becomes almost limitless." Remembering this in the skin of a Negro, I saw that it summed up the racist fallacy and its effects on all Negroes.

Later, as I made my way slowly through the more deprived areas of the Deep South, I learned some of those burningly shameful contradictions that Negro Catholics have to face. If it is painful to see that your country does not practice what it preaches, it is infinitely more painful to see that the Catholic Church does not. Though we deny that segregation exists in the Catholic Church, it does in effect exist.

I learned the humiliating protocol. In areas where there was no Negro Catholic church, it was made clear to me that I had better attend that one and no other. In areas where no provision existed, I attended a "white" church. But I was instructed by Negro Catholics to sit at the back of the church. If I wanted to receive Christ, I waited until the last white person had received Him and had returned to his seat before I approached the altar rail. Otherwise, I was warned, I would risk being passed at the altar rail. Negroes are constantly affronted by this. It either drives them deeper into the faith or it drives them away.

How can the Catholic Church be God-centered and yet practice this sort of segregation which it denounces as a "grave sin"? The point was clear. The Church did not practice this sort of segregation—this was the practice of bad Catholics, pure and simple. They persisted in a sin which their religion abominated.

Knowing this, however, was strangely poor consolation. In such areas, the blessed illusion of sanctuary within the Catholic Church was shattered. We were hurt there in our deepest selves.

Negroes were, in effect, second-class Catholics, as they were deemed second-class everything else. It was the same for all other Christian religions, of course, but that did not help either.

And when Negroes heard priests and bishops quietly explain their hesitancy to repudiate such attitudes "for fear of alienating souls," we knew they were referring to the souls of prejudiced white Catholics. And we wondered why they appeared to have so little "fear" of alienating the souls of Negroes.

How did otherwise decent white Christians justify such things?

They said: "Why Negroes are more comfortable in their place. They like it that way. It's a kindness really." I never heard a Negro say such a thing or in any way act as though he liked it that way. One of the greatest problems was the white man's willingness to solve all Negroes' problems according to the white man's comforts.

This was true in the North, South, East, and West.

In many rural areas and small towns, the "wonderfully harmonious relations" whites claimed to enjoy with Negroes resembled those one might enjoy with an animal beaten into utter submission. Here we knew that if we did not grin and say "Yes," to everything the white man wanted, we would be taught a lesson. We "accommodated," but when we went home in the evenings, we wept and said how could the white man twist his mind enough to think this death of our manhood, our hopes, and our dignity—this slavery—was for our own good.

As a stranger in their midst, I was taken in by Negroes and treated with the sort of protective tenderness that comes only from those who have suffered to the point of despair. One night, I watched a mother feed mashed yellow beans in Carnation milk to bright-eyed youngsters who did not yet know that doors into wonderlands of education and justice and employment opportunity were barred to them. They reminded me of my own children who could enter all of those doors. And I wondered how any human parent could tolerate a System that arbitrarily marked my children for privilege and these children for deprivation.

I said to myself: "We are not that evil. It's because we don't know, we don't understand what a killing thing it would be to look into your children's eyes and know they didn't have a chance." I told myself that we would shout our outrage if anyone advocated that we physically maim these children. Yet we daily implicated ourselves in the vaster crime that saw them spiritually maimed.

At that moment, I saw the lamp lit wretchedness in sharp focus, saw my hosts' faces flattened of all expression, dulled of hope or enthusiasm. I saw my black hands clenched in my lap and was torn to remember that I was once white. And I realized, with sickening horror, that we whites have permitted ourselves to allow fellow human beings to be turned into burnt-out shells who sat with me in that shanty. What great thing have we gained that was worth making them pay this kind of price?

These were people of quality. With education, the incentives of fair employment, a chance at human dignity, all of this would have been different. But we had condoned the System that deprived them of any chance to fulfill themselves. And then, unbearable irony, we had attributed their nonfulfillment to some imagined racial defect.

I could not understand how Negroes resisted the temptation to hate. They have a remarkable record for resisting subversion, for manifesting a deep love of country. But this is a love of what the country is *supposed to be*, the "American Dream"—not what it is where racism dominates. No, even in despair, Negroes could resist the temptation to hate whites, and this for two reasons.

First, they understood clearly what whites were only beginning to understand—that whites are as helplessly entrapped in the System as Negroes. Second, they believed their misery came from the "white trash" and that the trash, though powerful and unscrupulous, were a minority as oppressive and painful to the "good whites" as to the Negroes.

They seldom met these whites, but were sure they were there and could be counted on to behave correctly and to call for justice. A handful of them had stood up and been counted.

Lillian Smith, that great and brave Georgia writer of prophetic vision, had warned that those who embraced the strangely shallow dream of white supremacy were killers of the American dream of a society based on freedom, equality, and justice—and these whites who spoke such truths had been ostracized by racist reprisals.

Since I returned to white society on December 15, 1959, much of this has changed—and continues to change now in the autumn of 1963. The changes are so drastic that those who knew the South ten years ago, or even two years ago, are misinformed if they rely on that information or on what gets reported in the white press today.

Can the wounds be healed? Is death the only effective educator?

We go on speaking of gradualism, but in the skin of a Negro and through his eyes, it has become obvious that gradualism can stretch into eternity. We go on speaking of Negro crime, when Negroes know that these are not crimes of Negroes, but the crimes of men, the crimes of the ghetto where we have so long forced them to remain.

Yet we go on in the euphoric illusion of progress, while the Negro community wonders why. Can we draw love out of this cauldron of growing hatred, before it dehumanizes all of us? It is a moral problem, and unless we attack it at this level, we have no chance of evading the nation-wide explosion that must occur.

If Negroes have been embittered by the "white man's Christianity," they have been made deeply cynical by the "white man's politics." Demagogues have ridden to political power through appeals to popular prejudice and racist vilification. National political leaders have talked timidly about justice and acted even more timidly to implement it. White men have consistently decided what they think Negroes want, what is good for them, and how their problems should be solved—but always according to the white man's lights.

Even in inter group councils, Negroes are seldom allowed to choose their own representatives. The whites choose those Negroes whom they want on the councils. As one Negro minister put it: "They always talk for us and to us but never *with* us."

In the early days of the Kennedy Administration, despite some implementation that appeared radical to segregationists, Negroes viewed the government's refusal to "go all the way" as merely more tokenism. There lingered the suspicion that the government's stance was a matter of political maneuver rather than statesmanship. After so many disappointments with past presidents, few dared hope that President Kennedy's affirmations of right would stand the acid tests that would prove them true principles. When the showdown came, would he relax into the safety of nonaction or would he act as a man of principle? The showdown clearly came during the recent Alabama crisis. For the first time in history, a President spoke on the matter of civil rights without equivocation, and he followed through with a civil rights bill that had the ring of authentic statesmanship.

"We face a moral crisis in this country and as a people," President Kennedy said. "It cannot be met by repressive police action. It cannot be left to increased demonstrations in the streets. It cannot be quieted by token moves or talks. It is time to act in the Congress, in your state and local legislative body, and, above all, in your daily lives."

The president did not speak of Negroes as Negroes but as men, as citizens. He made no mention of the "Negro Problem" but spoke clearly of America's problem.

"A great change is at hand," he said, "and our task, our obligation, is to make that revolution, the change, peaceful and constructive for all." He was giving leadership and asking for leadership at the regional, the sectional, the local, and the individual level.

The issues are clear, and they have been clearly stated: we must choose to embrace the sanity of justice, or we will perish as a nation in the insanity of violence.

Negroes and most whites, surely, realize that we hang in the balance now.

Yet the President's eloquent words have been obstreperously repudiated by the Southern bloc, with a veritable orgy of question-begging epithets that any unprejudiced twelve-year-old could recognize as such.

Religion, in the eyes of many, has been a failure. When asked what he thought of the contributions of Christian ministers to the solution of our racist problems in the Deep South, white journalist P.D. East replied, "Very damn little. I always thought ministers of God were supposed to be leaders, not followers."

Many religious leaders have remained silent out of fear of precipitating violence. Ministers of the Protestant faiths have often remained silent because they knew they would be put out by their congregations, which would demand ministers with the "right kind of religion."

The growing sentiment, however, suggests that our time now in the early 1960s has become so critical that ministers must speak up and attempt to clear the consciences of their congregations and deal with the consequences without fear of reprisal.

In Mississippi, twenty-eight Methodists ministers spoke up and six were fired. Quakers, Presbyterians, Episcopalians, and many others have spoken up and have suffered the consequences. Among Catholics, the archbishops of Atlanta and New Orleans have been notable exceptions to a dreary picture. But the scandal of silence prevails in most churches. There are many reasons for this silence. Church leaders are in a difficult position where almost any overt movement could create chaos. However, we must face the painful fact that to Negroes these reasons are obscure at best, and the silence feels more like racism than Christian concern.

We are being subverted by expediency and compromise faster than we are being converted to ethical principles and wisdom. We are faced with two basic alternatives. We can look beyond the accident of skin color and view one another simply as human beings and we can join together in repudiating every injustice suffered by every citizen. Or we can deny the humanity that lies beneath our skins and set about the insane business of killing one another.

—1963

Malcolm X

Malcolm X was assassinated on a warm wintry Sunday, February 21, 1965. Although he was shot repeatedly in the presence of hundreds of witnesses at a meeting in New York's Audubon Ballroom, his murder remains a mystery. Grueling detective work and careful research by investigative reporters have failed to reveal who ordered the murder of one of the most famous men in history. In fact the trial of the three men accused of killing Malcolm was so poorly covered by the media that most people do not even know if they were proven guilty or what sentences they received.

In his recent book, *The Death and Life of Malcolm X*, Peter Goldman has thoroughly investigated the final years of Malcolm's life, his assassination, and the events leading to the arrests and trial of the trigger men. This fascinating study contains a great deal of material never before published. The author reveals the profoundly religious aspects of Malcolm's adult life. He traces the transformation in attitudes about Malcolm who was often viewed as a dangerous hate monger by blacks and whites alike during his life, but who has gradually come to be considered a kind of saint over the years since his assassination.

A year before he was killed, Malcolm was asked by a Swedish TV interviewer when he was first hurt by segregation, as though Malcolm's anger could be traced to a single incident.

"When I was born," Malcolm said. "I was born in a segregated hospital of a segregated mother and a segregated father."

The reporter wanted something more specific, some incident that had earned Malcolm's discontent.

"The first was when we were living in Lansing, Michigan, in an integrated neighborhood. One night I woke up and found the house on fire. The good Christians of the neighborhood had come and set the house afire. The second was when my father was found under a streetcar where he had been thrown by the good Christians—that's my second. You want my third and fourth and fifth and sixth and seventh?"

Malcolm X was born Malcolm Little in Omaha, Nebraska, May 19, 1925. He was the son of Rev. Earl Little, a black-skinned Baptist preacher from rural Georgia and Louise, a light-skinned West Indian. His father was a huge man and Malcolm himself grew to a height of six foot three. From his mother he got his light color, "a reddish-brown somewhere between copper and *café au lait*; black people call the shade 'mariny,'" writes Goldman. "I make the white man feel his guilt," Malcolm would say. "When he looks at this mariny face of mine, he knows what he did to my grandmother."

Malcolm's father was devoted to Marcus Garvey, the first of Harlem's great black nationalists. He was known, as Malcolm was, as a "crazy nigger." Because of his refusal to bow down, Earl Little was driven out of Omaha, had his home burned in Lansing, beaten almost to death and then thrown under a trolley which killed him.

"Malcolm was six then," Goldman reports. "His boyhood memories thereafter were of poverty and days dizzy with hunger; of boiled dandelion greens for dinner and orange peels for dessert when you could beg them from the neighbors; of the family disintegrating—or being disintegrated, Malcolm always thought—by the clumsy cruelties of the welfare bureaucracy. Louise Little, hurt and cornered, wound up in a mental hospital, the other children in various foster homes—and Malcolm, stormy and rebellious, in a detention in Mason, Michigan, awaiting transfer to reform school."

Malcolm did not actually go to reform school. He charmed the lady who ran the home into letting him stay. He went to school in Mason where he appears to have made straight A's, joined the debating club and was elected president of the seventh grade.

In the eighth grade everything collapsed for the young student. He came up against the hard fact that no matter how hard he worked, how brilliantly he performed, a black in those days dared not have very high ambitions. "When I was young," Malcolm said, "the only thing you could dream about becoming was a good waiter or a good busboy or a good shoeshine man…"

After the eighth grade, Malcolm dropped out and took to the streets. He soon moved to Boston, got a zoot suit, had his hair conked and held a series of petty jobs. He got himself a white girlfriend and thought he loved white people in those days. "I was trying as hard as I could do be white," he said.

Still in his teens, but tall and big enough to pass for a man, Malcolm was tired of the nickel and dime jobs and moved into Harlem where he got involved in selling drugs, running numbers, pimping and armed robbery. He became known in the streets as Detroit Red or Big Red. "He was a bad-ass cat, a murder-mouthing blood with an evil temper and a piece jammed in his belt to back it up," writes Goldman. Although he was not medically an addict, he stayed high on opium, hashish, reefers, cocaine. He never shot heroin, as he said, because he intended to sell to the chumps who used the needle.

He finally had to leave Harlem to escape not only the police but the enemies he had made in the streets. He returned to Boston, formed a burglary gang with his former white girlfriend and her sister and two black friends. They were caught in a robbery and put on trial. Malcolm believed he got a much stiffer sentence than he otherwise would have because of his association with the white girls. "The judge told me to my face, 'This will teach you to stay away from white girls.'" The girls were sentenced from one to five years. Malcolm got eight to ten. Shortly before his 21st birthday, he began his long term, of which he served six years and five months in three Massachusetts penitentiaries. He was known inside the walls as Satan—an incorrigible hard-timer, with his mind, as he later put it, in a "fog bag" and his gut in a state of permanent mutinous rage.

In prison he began cold-bloodedly to "rehabilitate" himself. He needed better instruments simply to survive in the world, and he saw knowledge as one of those instruments. A fellow inmate called Bimbi got Malcolm interested in books and correspondence courses in English, Latin and German. At first his studies had no real meaning or purpose except to help him make it in the world. Soon, they took on profound meaning. Malcolm's conversion to the Lost-Found Nation was instantaneous and blinding, and it transformed his life almost immediately. It came from his younger brother, Reginald, who told Malcolm that he had it on the authority of the Honorable Elijah Muhammad, who had learned it from Allah Himself, that white people are the devil. Reginald's statement made it possible for him to convert Malcolm "in five minutes," Malcolm said. "Despite my many experiences with whites, the fact that I had grown up with whites and was reared by whites and had socialized with whites in every form of their life, and even though I was in prison, I still respected whites. But when my brother told me that God had taught Mr. Elijah Muhammad that the white race was a race of devils, my eyes came open on the spot."

Malcolm's conversion was an authentic one that completely changed his life, gave it direction and meaning. He was, in the language of the Nation of Islam, being resurrected from the grave of life outside the faith. He spent his remaining years in prison in endless labor of study. He copied out the dictionary word for word on writing tablets. He read incessantly at night until he damaged his eyes, straining them to study in the dim light from the prison corridors. Eventually Elijah Muhammad himself tutored Malcolm by mail in the sacraments of Black Islam. Malcolm read the Greeks, Hegel and Kant, Shakespeare and Schopenhauer and Nietzsche, philology and etymology, "searching in all of it for wisdom and for evidence against white folks." Language became an obsession as he grew to realize the meaning and power of words. He learned to pray. He dropped all vices and pleasures, completely cutting himself away from his past.

When Malcolm came out of prison in 1952, he went directly into the Nation of Islam—a small community at the time of 400 scattered among store-front mosques and front-parlor missions in Detroit, Chicago, Washington, Harlem and a few other places. Malcolm confirmed his commitment by abandoning the "slave name" Little and receiving the "X" which, as he explained, announced what you had been and what you had now become—"Ex-smoker, Ex-drinker, Ex-Christian, Ex-slave." Malcolm quickly threw himself into work as a Nation builder with the zeal of a convert. He rose rapidly to assistant minister in Detroit, then minister in Boston and Philadelphia.

The devotion between Elijah Muhammad and his disciple was total. It quickly became a father-son relationship. Malcolm felt that the "Messenger" had literally picked him up from the ruins of his life and made him a person of dignity and worth. In 1958 he sought Elijah Muhammad's blessing on his marriage to Betty.

During the years when he had become famous and was revered by his followers as much as Elijah Muhammad, when it was Malcolm X who attracted the thousands to hear his talks, he would invariably push his mentor to the forefront. "I am not the author of anything I say," he would insist. "I am only repeating that which has been taught me by the Honorable Elijah Muhammad."

In Malcolm's time, the rules for life among the Lost-Founds were very strict. Muslims were limited to one meal a day, though they could take coffee or fruit juice at any time, and they were required to fast three days a month. The women of the Nation were expected to be good, chaste and dutiful housewives. The men, called The Fruit of Islam, were expected to protect and care for their women. The rules so arranged their lives that they spent as much time as possible together and as little time as possible in the "grave" (the world outside). They had services Sunday afternoon and meetings at the mosque five nights a week. They tended to spend their free time visiting one another. The Muslims believed in clean minds, in clean bodies, daily bathing and washing before prayers. "The rigorous morality extended to language (Malcolm wouldn't even say 'hell' unless powerfully moved)," Goldman points out.

Malcolm thrived and grew in the life, in the world of the Nation. He helped organize the newspapers, conducted study groups and rose to national prominence. In a sense he was two men: the one known to the world as a terrifyingly brilliant critic of white injustices who believed all whites were Satan; the other a deeply committed religious leader and teacher, a gentle man, an aristocrat, warm and human.

With growing fame, his faith began to be troubled. "Islam was a world for Malcolm, and, for most of his years in Elijah

Muhammad's service, he was secure and comfortable inside it," writes Goldman. "But the larger world outside discovered him, and he was drawn to it—to its complexity, its sophistication, its very worldliness." He became friends with many prominent people of his day—Muhammad Ali, Ossie Davis and Ruby Dee, John Oliver Killens and Dick Gregory, Kenneth Clark and James Farmer, Sidney Poitier, Percy Sutton and Adam Clayton Powell. Malcolm never cheapened these friendships by displaying them. He never tried to convert them and they did not try to convert him. But his world was widening. They influenced Malcolm to be more aware and to become part of the larger black community.

Neither Malcolm nor the Black Muslims ever advocated aggressive violence, despite the impression given by the media, but they did advocate self-defense. Whereas Rev. Martin Luther King, Jr. advocated nonviolent resistance, redemptive suffering, turning the other cheek, Malcolm advocated striking back if attacked. "When the Japanese attacked Pearl Harbor," Malcolm pointed out, "Uncle Sam didn't say, 'Forget Pearl Harbor.'" He felt that simply to go on taking abuse was degrading to any man. On the other hand, the Muslims believed that Allah would punish the offenders, and counted on it. However, when blacks were abused, when Black Muslims were murdered and the Fruit of Islam waited for the word to kill the white devil, Elijah Muhammad would send word, usually through Malcolm, to wait, to do nothing, to let Allah take care of it.

So, with conflicts arising from his contacts with the world and from within the Nation, Malcolm began to doubt. He also was aware that there were white Muslims in the world. How to reconcile this fact with the Black Muslim doctrine in America that all whites were devils? At first Malcolm simply suppressed his doubts. Doubt was not tolerated by Black Muslims. To express doubt was called "seed planting"—and the Muslims detested the "bad seed planter." Malcolm struggled against his doubts. The Nation was his world, and nothing was more fearful than being cast out. The children of Allah referred to such banishment as "going back to the grave."

Another problem for Malcolm, as he became a world figure, lay in his desire to be recognized as part of the black leadership. He was never called to any of the conferences of black leaders, largely due to the fact that his public reputation as a "hate-monger" made people afraid of him. Also, Elijah Muhammad continually restrained him from any participation in the "Movement." According to Goldman:

> The Nation's policy was strict abstention, partly out of a fine ideological scorn for everything the civil-rights movement aspired to, partly out its own deepening, don't-rock-the-boat conservatism at the top. Malcolm obeyed, increasingly unhappily. He saw that the locus of history was in the streets, however misguided the official struggle there seemed to him, and both his energy and his *amour-propre* impelled him to be where the action was.

During his last days as a Black Muslim, Malcolm told author Louis Lomax: "The Messenger [Elijah Muhammad] has seen God. He was with Allah and was given divine patience with the devil. He is willing to wait for Allah to deal with this devil. Well, sir, the rest of us Black Muslims have not seen God, we don't have this gift of divine patience with the devil. The younger Black Muslims want to see some action."

As the Nation had grown and become wealthy, in part through Malcolm's own ardent efforts and devotion, organizational bureaucracy had inevitably crept in. The top management was increasingly uneasy about Malcolm, and perhaps jealous of his prestige. In a sense, he remained pure, priestly and ardent at a time when the Nation's leadership had become comfortable and wanted things calm. He was further distressed by what he saw as the creeping capitalism of the Nation, which had "a taste for creature comfort that, so he and his circle believed, had seeped down from the theocrats in Chicago to the pettiest functionaries in the mosques," explains Goldman. "Malcolm lived modestly, gave all his earnings to The Nation, and died broke. He believed that those who sought too many comforts paid with a 'certain loss of limberness and soul.'"

When the Nation's newspaper, *Muhammad Speaks*, was moved to Chicago it began to play down Malcolm's roles as the "star" of the Black Muslims. One issue spoke at great length about Elijah Mohammad and one of his rallies and only mentioned in passing "Out of town ministers included...Malcolm Shabazz, New York (Mosque # 7)." With all of these strains, the break was soon inevitable. It was precipitated by rumors of scandal in Elijah Muhammad's personal relationships with some of his secretaries, a scandal that horrified Malcolm and which he tried to keep from becoming public knowledge; although after the break, he no longer suppressed the disclosures.

"I believed in him [Elijah Mohammad] as a man 100 percent," Malcolm said. "I believed he was divine, divinely taught and divinely guided. And it was only when he found himself confronted with a moral question which he could not face up to as a man that it made me begin to doubt him, not only someone divine but it made me doubt him as a man. And in the face of that I began to analyze everything else he taught."

The occasion for Malcolm's silencing came when, after a lecture, he was asked about the assassination of President John F. Kennedy. He called the president's death a case of "the chickens come home to roost." His statement was noised around the world and it sounded almost inhumanly callous. Malcolm explained that he had simply meant that the president's death was the inevitable consequence of a climate of hate and violence in America, the same thing many whites had said. He was reproved by The Nation immediately on the grounds that his statement was—no matter what his intentions—in "bad taste." Elijah Muhammad ordered Malcolm to go on running the mosque, but to be silent for 90 days—to make no talks and grant no interviews.

His off-the-cuff statement not only discredited him in the public eye, but it provided his enemies within the Nation with the means of ruining him. "He sensed that he would be cast back into the world, which was to say the grave; he saw that he had set himself up for it. He was exhausted. His nerves were shot," writes Goldman. Near the end of his time of silence, some of the Muslims from the Harlem Mosque came to him and confided that they had been ordered by a Muslim officer to assassinate him. As Goldman explains, Elijah Muhammad stated that no Muslim would harm Malcolm since they all believed that Allah would sufficiently destroy him; but the word could be passed that it might be well for someone to assassinate him. This is apparently what happened in February of 1964. He had only a year to live, a year in which death approached him like an animal stalking its victim.

Although Malcolm detached himself from The Nation, or was thrown out, his religious convictions remained profound. His separation freed him from some of his concepts which he could no longer accept. One of these was its absolute doctrine that all whites were Satan incarnate. He had already had to face the fact that some whites he had met were not devils he could and did respect, some he even liked. He was sometimes deeply touched by the open students on the campuses where he appeared. "To have reached a point where one lost sight of color was, for a Black Muslim, to have sunk in error," writes Goldman. Malcolm realized this and he tried to handle it by suppressing his realization that at least some whites of his acquaintance were "not nearly so terrifying an enemy as Satan." He drifted, with his religious faith, toward "true Islam."

Some orthodox Muslims in America suggested that Malcolm get in contact with Dr. Mahmoud Youssef Shawarbe, an Egyptian learned in Islam at the time directing the Islamic Center of New York. Dr. Shawarbe liked Malcolm immediately. "He was a thorough gentleman, full of glamour and humor," Shawarbe said. But the doctor was affronted by Malcolm's "cultish visions of God and the devil." He told Malcolm that Islam was a religion of peace and love, and he read Malcolm this verse from the Koran: "Muslims are all brothers regardless of their color or race." This was elementary teaching, something Malcolm certainly knew, but Shawarbe says Malcolm jumped to his feet and asked him to read it again. He did, noting that during the second reading Malcolm stood shivering and weeping. After weeks of tutoring, Dr. Shawarbe made arrangements with the Saudi Arabian government for Malcolm to make the orthodox Muslim's obligatory pilgrimage to Mecca.

That pilgrimage was a revelation for Malcolm. For the first time in his experience, considerations of color could simply disappear. Accompanying him on the pilgrimage, he said, "was every shade, every complexion, every type of color. And all of these were under the same tent. And on this pilgrimage you ate with your hands—everyone eats from the same plate—so this involved me in a situation where I was eating from the same plate with people who in this country would be considered white. I found myself drinking from the same glass, and sleeping on the same cot, and praying on the same rug with people who in this country would definitely be classified as white people."

"To me," he said later," a white man had always been a white man—this was my blanket classification. But I had to finally reach the conclusion the thing that made them different there was the fact that they had accepted the oneness of God, and in accepting the oneness of God, their intelligence demanded that they also accept the oneness of humanity." Although this realization was critical to Malcolm's growth in his religion, it did not mean that he had softened his views about whites in America, who practiced "conscious racism."

"All Malcolm saw in Mecca," Goldman points out, "and all his various messages conceded, was the humanity of white people, nothing more. A white person, if he was capable of brotherhood with blacks, could not after all be the devil. But in Malcolm's sight, white people in America remained guilty of collective and historic devilishness toward blacks."

He went on pilgrimage as Malcolm X and he returned as El-Hajj Malik El-Shabazz, an accredited Sunni Muslim. Before coming back to America, however, Malcolm went on to Africa in the hope of strengthening ties with black leaders there. His major goal was to line up sponsors in Africa who would take the case of American blacks before the United Nations. He was received as an honored guest everywhere he went. "He moved with dazzling ease among men of power and affairs, as though he had been doing it all his life. Africa's rulers impressed Malcolm, but it was Africa itself that enthralled him. He hopped from capital to capital across the north and west, alone and, to the dismay of friends and admirers he saw along the way, unguarded," writes

Goldman. Although he gradually came to realize that in spite of his overwhelming welcome by Africa's leaders, they were not going to make his case to the United Nations, because too many of them were dependent on American aid, he refused to give up hope that he could eventually bring his plan to fruition and he had no time for his disappointments.

During his visit to Ghana, where he spent much time with Julian Mayfield and Maya Angelou, who said, "He was expansive. He was open. He was learning. He was no longer in love with a position—he was in love with truth. When she shuffled off that Black Muslim coil, he shuffled the whole thing off. You'd tell him something, and he would say, 'That's a very good point. I see. I was wrong about that.' And he was absolutely as strong in his new position as in his old one. He had no loyalty to old misconceptions."

Malcolm returned to America in May and tried to explain his new flexibility to his old following, but many were dismayed that he had tempered his views. He hoped to offer an alternative leadership to those who could not go the Black Muslim way, or the Martin Luther King way. And after the glories of Africa, he returned to trouble, to renewed threats on his life and to a battle with the Black Muslims, who considered him an unforgivable heretic and defector. Malcolm fought back. He used every means at his disposal, including exposing Elijah Muhammad's soiled reputation. Meanwhile he was constantly being denounced in the newspaper *Muhammad Speaks*. He now required a bodyguard everywhere he went, and he bought weapons to protect his family at home.

During the last year he spent more than half the time abroad. He returned to Cairo where he was certified as a Muslim minister. The world Muslim League made him its representative in America. These credentials were important to one who felt he had harmed many black people as a Black Muslim minister. "For twelve long years," he wrote in a letter to the *New York Times*, "I lived in the narrow-minded confines of the 'straitjacket world' created by my strong belief that Elijah Muhammad was a messenger direct from God Himself and I shall never rest until I have undone the harm I did to so many well-meaning, innocent

Negroes who through my own evangelistic zeal now believe in him even more fanatically and more blindly than I did."

Added to his fear of assassination was his certainty that he was being pursued by the U.S. government because of his attempts to get America condemned before the United Nations. While in Africa he became violently ill one night after dinner at the Nile Hilton and was hospitalized. "He suspected that he had been poisoned and guessed that American agents had done it," writes Goldman, who found no evidence for these suspicions. The U.S. government was not very interested in Malcolm's trip until later, when in fact it did put him under surveillance.

When Malcolm returned to Ghana the second time, his mood was different. His United Nation's case was, he now saw, not going to materialize. Maya Angelou described this somber mood. "There was a sense of—not desperation, you know, but it was like the hand of fate was on him." Malcolm was worried about the surveillance put on him by the U.S. government. He told Julian Mayfield that if anything happened to him in America "they shouldn't necessarily think it was solely the doing of the Black Muslims." But if he worried about surveillance abroad, he was even more worried about returning to Harlem. His friends in Africa were equally worried about him. "All of us begged him to stay," Maya Angelou recalls. "We were afraid for his life…We said, 'Just spend six months here, let that jazz cool off. We told him to bring Betty and the children. We told him he could give lectures anywhere. We told him any government would have taken him in."

Malcolm did come back to America to face the final months of nerve-wracking threats that almost led him to a nervous collapse. He was convinced that he would be killed, and probably in a public place. His bodyguards stayed with him constantly even though Malcolm knew that nothing could prevent his death if people were determined that he should die. Some of his oldest and closest friends moved away from him. Charles Kenyatta, who had been one of his most faithful friends, felt that Malcolm had chosen other friends and other ways. He did not come back to Malcolm until the end, when Malcolm announced to him simply, "I'm a dead man."

In February of 1965 Malcolm made one final brief trip to England. He was supposed to speak in France, but the French government refused to allow him into the country. He was furious, thinking the CIA might have persuaded the French to bar him. This incident led to wide speculation that the CIA might have ordered his death. Goldman rather thoroughly traces down the evidence for this belief and finds little to support it. On February 13 he flew back to New York, having already dispatched a letter to Julian Mayfield asking him to see that some African government took in Betty and the children if he were murdered. The following Saturday he told his biographer, Alex Haley, that he had changed his mind about blaming the Black Muslims if he were assassinated. He had been deeply afflicted by his expulsion from France. He felt that Muslims would actually do the killing, but as trigger men for whom? For The Nation of Islam? For the FBI? For the CIA?

Malcolm stayed in New York that Saturday night, in a room on the 12th floor of the New York Hilton. At eight the next morning, he was awakened by the phone. When he picked it up he heard a voice say, "Wake up, Brother." Then the phone clicked off. Malcolm got up and dressed. He called Betty and asked her to bring the children to his rally at the Audubon Ballroom that afternoon. He checked out of his room and made his way carefully to the Audubon.

Only one young policeman stood outside the ballroom, whereas usually there were a number. The police, in fact, had received intelligence reports only two weeks before indicating that Malcolm was in serious danger of being killed. Today, however, one of Malcolm's senior officers had asked the police to remain invisible and the remainder of the 20-man detail was hidden in Columbia Presbyterian Medical Center across the street. Aside from the officer at the door, two more were inside with walkie-talkies and orders to alert the others if anything happened. Malcolm's own guards watched the inside, but they had been ordered by Malcolm not to carry weapons that day, and security was not very tight.

Malcolm sat in the small dressing room off the stage as the hall began to fill up. A number of guests had been invited to share the platform with him, but for various reasons none of them could come. Malcolm looked at the empty chairs on the stage, slumped in his own chair backstage, then jumped up and paced the floor. "He was more tense than I'd ever seen him," said one of his friends. "He just lost control of himself completely. I never saw him do that before."

Benjamin Goodman, Malcolm's long time friend, was asked to give the "opening up" speech—something he had done often in the past. Malcolm sat in the room while Goodman talked to the crowd, telling the little group in the back room that something felt wrong out there. When he stood up to go on, Goodman saw him in the doorway and hurried into his windup: "I present one who is wiling to put himself on the line for you, a man who would give his life for you…" He had not meant anything special by this, had had no premonition of anything, it was just something one said. Malcolm strode onto the empty stage, passing Goodman who was coming off. The audience applauded a full minute, bringing a slow smile to Malcolm's face. When they quieted, he gave them the Muslim greeting, "*As-salaam Alaikum.*" "*Wa-alaikum salaam,*" they shouted in response.

At that moment, the crowd's attention was distracted when two men in the crowd got into an argument and jumped to their feet. "What are you doing in my pockets, man?" one of them shouted. "Get your hand out of my pocket." The two guards at the foot of the stage were drawn away from Malcolm to the disturbance.

"Hold it, hold it, Brothers. "Let's be cool," Malcolm said, his last words drowned out by the roar of a shotgun blast. The gun was fired by a man coming at him with a sawed-off double-barrel 12-gauge Higgins shotgun. Author Peter Goldman describes the scene in exacting detail:

> "A dozen double-O buckshot pellets, each the diameter of
> a .32-calibre bullet, ripped through the plywood lectern as
> if it were paper and made a perfectly patterned seven-inch
> circle of holes dead center on Malcolm's chest. Malcolm's
> hands flew halfway up. His eyes rolled back. There was
> blood on his face and his shirt front. He rocked on his

heels and toppled over backward, crashing into two of the empty guest chairs. His head thudded hard on the floor. The man with the shotgun fired his second load."

The two men who had been arguing to distract the guards from Malcolm's position quickly mingled with the frantic crowd, rushed forward and began emptying their pistols into the fallen body of Malcolm X. In the turmoil, the man wielding the shotgun tossed it aside and escaped in the crowd of 400 people. One of his companions also escaped. The third was caught by the crowd and rescued from their furious beating by the police outside.

Malcolm lay on the stage were he had fallen. Betty had fought her way to the stage and stood beside him, along with others who attempted to revive him with mouth-to-mouth resuscitation. Some of the brothers had rushed across the street to the Medical Center, got a stretcher and brought it back. They lifted Malcolm on to it and ran down the aisle shouting "Get out of the way or we'll kill you."

At the medical center, doctors worked 15 minutes in a desperate attempt to save Malcolm's life, but it was hopeless. The shotgun blast had destroyed his heart, punctured his lungs and hit his spine. After a short time a man came downstairs and announced to the group in the waiting room, "The gentleman you know as Malcolm X is dead."

The police already held one young man, Talmadge Hayer, in custody. They had difficulty with the investigation because many of the witnesses simply refused to cooperate with them. They finally caught two other suspects, Norman 3X Butler and Thomas 15X Johnson.

After lying in state for most of the week and being viewed by thousands of mourners, Malcolm was buried Saturday, February 17, 1965. The funeral home where the body lay in state had received bomb threats almost daily. The chapel from which he was buried also received bomb threats. Police were everywhere, fearing that Harlem might explode at any moment.

They buried Malcolm in Ferncliff Cemetery. The bronze plaque read simply: "EL-HAJJ MALIK EL-SHABAZZ.

It took almost a year to bring the three suspects to trial, which opened on January 12, 1966. The three suspects were found guilty and sentenced to life in prison. Although all of them offered alibis, they were too flimsy to hold up under investigation. None of the men could be made to reveal who ordered the murder.

Many theories have been held. Some have thought that it was an inside job ordered by some member of Malcolm's own organization. Many still believe that it was connected with the government, a theory that has been refurbished among black intellectuals by revelations of FBI sabotage of various civil rights and militant organizations—along with the facts that Malcolm was under surveillance, his talks recorded, his phones bugged.

In the prosecutor's summary before the jury, he said the very brazenness of the act suggested the answer.

> Ordinarily, if a person makes up his mind to kill somebody, he does it in secret. He doesn't want any witnesses available. It's done in the dead of night, secretly, quietly. But when you consider the evidence... whoever did it chose to do it in the presence of 400 people in broad daylight in a public room. Is it abusing our common sense to suggest that it was done deliberately in the presence of these people as an object lesson to Malcolm's followers that this is what can happen and what will happen?"

The prosecutor did not have to answer his own rhetorical question.

—1975

American Racism in the Sixties

The only thing necessary for the triumph of evil,
is for good men to do nothing.

—Edmund Burke

Your prayers and hymns, your sermons and thanksgivings, with
all your religious parade and solemnity, are mere bombast, fraud,
deception, impiety and hypocrisy—a thin veil to cover up the
crimes which would disgrace a nation of savages.

—Frederick Douglass, July 4, 1852

Blaming the Victim

On Passion Sunday, 1968, Dick Gregory and I walked
with the campus minister toward the chapel of the University
of the Pacific in Stockton, California. The minister briefed us on
our schedule for the day.

Gregory glanced up at the sunlit façade of the chapel.
"God, I hate to go in these pagan temples of hypocrisy," he said
quietly.

Neither of us answered. There was nothing to answer.

I remembered a scene in the kitchen of St. Carthage's
rectory in Chicago where we talked through the night with a
group of priests serving slum parishes. Gregory told us how,
as a youngster, he had sought refuge in Catholic churches. "I'd
open the door and look in. If the church was empty, I'd go in
and sit—just to get away from the noise and stink of the slum—
just to be alone for awhile away from all that."

Now, the kind of edifices he had once considered places of sanctuary had become in his mind "pagan temples of hypocrisy."

We listened that Sunday to a liturgy that struck us as starkly personal.

"O God, sustain my cause, give me redress against a race that knows no piety, save me from a treacherous and cruel foe . . . ." A voice sent the words out over the speakers in the church. *"Deliver me, Lord, from my enemies."*

The glances we exchanged expressed clearly what we did not need to say; the "cruel and treacherous foe" for us was racism, quite particularly racism that hid behind the guise of religion. That cruel and treacherous foe had killed too many men and women whose lives had been connected with our lives.

". . . more, the hour is coming when those who kill you will claim to be serving God."

Who would be racism's next victim? Who would be the next to die physically from a bullet or a club? Or who would be the next to go through that kind of death that comes from calumny, character-assassination, blackmail? I listened to the sounds of the service. I wondered if others heard the words of the liturgy with the same personal recognition we did. Had any of them known the intimate grief of seeing friends and colleagues shot or beaten by racists who called themselves Christians?

Gregory, his bearded face skeletal from a long fast, looked at me and then leaned forward, his elbows on his knees, and stared at the floor between his feet. Was he remembering the victims? If so, which ones?

Father Morrisroe from Chicago who was shot in the back in the same shooting that killed Episcopal seminarian Jonathan Daniels?—both men guilty of nothing more than acts of mercy, but dismissed as "nigger lovers" in Mississippi. Tom Coleman, their admitted killer described as "a good family man," was acquitted in a trial that blamed the victim, that sought to prove him a sinner and his executioner innocent.

Was it Vernon Dahmer, murdered when his home was fire-bombed in Hattiesburg, Mississippi, in a holocaust that injured also his wife and daughter? The victim was blamed. He was a black man guilty of seeking civil rights. Did the murderers claim to be serving God? Defense-fund benefit dinners were held for the accused killers and reported in the newspaper as "a tremendous success." According to the newspaper, tickets for the fund-raising dinners read: "Proceeds to defend our white Christian citizens being charged and persecuted under the so-called Civil Rights Act."

Was it James Chaney, Michael Schwerner and Andrew Goodman, a black Catholic and two Jews, brutalized and executed near Philadelphia, Mississippi, after being entrapped in an act of "mercy" by a group of "white Christians," one of whom was a preacher who prayed before the three men were murdered?

Was it Clyde Kennard, that brilliant black man who served in the armed forces of his country in Germany and Korea, fighting in defense of "American rights and liberties," and who then returned to his homeland, sought to claim just one of those rights—the right to complete his education—and was martyred by men who called themselves "good Christians." Dick Gregory had spent a great deal of money trying to save Kennard's life.

Was it Clark Cooper, Auburey Pollard and Fred Temple—beaten and murdered in the Algiers Motel in Detroit by men who, under the guise of love for law, order and virtue, reportedly said: "We're going to kill all you black-ass nigger pimps and throw you in the river," and who terrorized two women by stripping them, beating them and asking if they wanted to die first or to watch the men be killed and die afterward.

Was Gregory remembering these, or the many others who have died in similar ways? Or perhaps, like me, he thought of those who have been martyred without being physically destroyed, including the priests, nuns, ministers and rabbis attacked for seeking to implement their churches' teachings on racism and justice. I thought of the nuns who had gone to Selma, Alabama—Sisters I had known in their convents before they went and after they returned from Selma. Catholic racists deliberately contrived "documented proof" in the form of spurious photographs purporting to show that the Sisters were not nuns at all but whores from New Jersey hired to masquerade as nuns. These photographs were distributed among Catholics by Catholics who had to know they were spreading a lie but were willing to murder the reputation of nuns.

I remembered sitting in a rectory in an upper-class Oklahoma City parish with a young priest who had gone to Selma. His face blanked with disbelief as he told me of the animosity this had aroused in many of his parishioners. "I never really believed men who seemed to be such fine citizens could be so enslaved by these prejudices," he said. "What's happening to them? I get hate stares now, right in church, from people who wouldn't think of missing Mass. This morning one of the ladies who had received communion from my hand met me at the doorway after Mass. She refused to shake my hand. She looked me straight in the face and asked, 'How's your woman, Father?' It's been spread around that Selma was one big sex orgy. They're pretending we didn't go there out of conscience or for a principle, but because somebody promised us an experience with a black woman. What is all this? If these people were trash, I could understand it, but they're not, really."

Priests, ministers, rabbis, nuns were deliberately calumnied by Christians who had to defend their racist aberrations with such *ad hominen* attacks. Nearly all the churches have known these "old and ugly subtleties," as Adlai Stevenson called them, whereby men commit crimes under the guises of religion and patriotism.

Whose life would be taken next? What reputation murdered next?

Within a few days we knew. Martin Luther King was shot down in Memphis. It was not enough that his life was taken. Some men continued to murder his reputation after his death. A first principle of racism holds that racists always blame their victims.

Painful Truths about the System

White men often tell me what *one* black man or lady said to them, as though this represented the thoughts and feelings of all black people. White people think that black people think monolithically. I always advise these whites to ask the same question of twelve black people, and suggest they will probably get twelve different answers. Black Americans no more think monolithically than do white Americans. The very suggestion that black people think monolithically is viewed by many black people as one of those revelations of unconscious racism that so falsify truth and handicap communication. It is an attitude that lumps human individuals together into a group and then attaches group characteristics: Blacks think this way or act that way, or black people ought to think such and such a way. Black Americans, experiencing it daily, understand it as a frustrating element of the duality of viewpoint that destroys all hope of communication. This duality of viewpoint is a prime key to our difficulties. It is a first principle of anthropology that members of one cultural or ethnic group tend to regard those of another group as merely underdeveloped versions of themselves. This is almost universal and it is fundamentally racist. Churchmen appear particularly prone to this error, which accounts for the ineffectiveness of missionary activity.

This problem of an imprisoning and blinding culture expresses itself in what Edward Hall calls "the silent language"—a language by which men unknowingly express, through attitudes, springing from learned behavior patterns, truths that contradict their actual words, and of which they may be wholly unconscious. This silent language is an intrinsic element in the duality of viewpoint that persists between black and white Americans. The duality is grounded in racial and racist mythology so deeply inculcated in learned behavior patterns that men tend to call it human nature, which it is not at all. Black men meet this attitude constantly in encounters with even the best-intentioned white men who sincerely believe they are all for equality but who betray an illusion that blacks are underdeveloped versions of whites and must be helped to rise up to "our level." To black men, whose lives have forced them to become masterful interpreters of such nuances, this is so degrading it alienates immediately. We have the duality between what is sincerely professed and what is practiced.

In long experience, I have found only a handful of men who could break out of the prison of culture—in this case, of an essentially white culture—and who were capable of "thinking human" rather than "thinking white." One of the reasons a black man might speak with contempt for "the white man's God" is because too often what he hears as the word of God from the white man's mouth comes into his ears as a distortion of the truths taught him by his own life. He hears the white man talk about a theological definition of man as a sacred reality, and this without regard to race, color or creed. But then, where this makes sense to him, he hears in addition and from the same lips, all the paternalistic equivocations that separate "our black brothers" from other men, stand them up as a group somehow intrinsically different, *intrinsically Other*.

These contradictions are overwhelmingly evident to black men, and they are deeply insulting because part of their implication is that the black man cannot see through them, or perhaps even does not perceive them. As a result we have a long history of alienation because of a compromise that sought to avoid it. How many church leaders have warned against "pushing things too fast and in a manner that might alienate souls"? Black men used to hear that all the time; and they wondered at the obtuseness of it—the Church's fear that by being what it professed to be, it would alienate souls. Whose souls? Apparently the souls of prejudiced whites. Black people saw through it, saw that in going along with white prejudices, the Church apparently had little or no concern about alienating the souls of black people. If one happened to be black, was that somehow a different "sacred reality" from whites?

After a lifetime of such duality, and with the knowledge that it has gone on for generations, black men do not have very high hopes that white men will ever see clear in this. Because it is not new. White men appear to think that it is contemporary, to judge from the appeals for patience on the part of the black man, and their judgment that "such things take time." This is again part of the duality. It is new to the white man, but it is old, old to the black man, who has heard these things all through his life. He knows that militancy is not new. Over a hundred years ago black men were saying it "like it is" and publicly and loudly.

I am not suggesting that churches ever really wanted it that way. Part of the tragedy we witness today lies in the fact that no one really wants what is happening, but the duality of viewpoint has become so extreme that we are virtually two groups of citizens in possession of two different sets of information, moving into deeper quagmires of incomprehension, with white perceptions about the problems of black people lagging far behind black perceptions. An indication of this is found in the nearly universal refusal of white men to contradistinguish between militancy, black power and violence. White men use these terms almost interchangeably. Black men do not. Most black men have been driven to a stance of militancy, some find solutions in the concepts of Black Power. Again, none of this is new. We miss the point completely if we go on thinking that these are new and recent developments. They are continuous and degenerating. Because men did not listen to Frederick Douglass and those like him over a hundred years ago, we hear in today's streets what a young black man, with good cause, said to me in a rage meeting attended by his parents, fellow students and others from his community. "You go back, and you tell your friend Mr. Jesus Christ, and you tell your friend, Dr. Martin Luther King—shit." He had been grossly brutalized and subjected to injustice at the hands of local lawmakers, and no local white religiously-identifiable person or group had uttered a word of protest.

Anyone working to bridge the gap of incomprehension brought about by this duality of viewpoint faces an almost hopeless task. White men will think he is exaggerating, while black men will think he is understating the truth. White church leaders will reprimand him for not "stressing the good things the Church has done." Here the implications are dizzying. They can range anywhere from the belief that "we took them out of the jungles, civilized them, gave them a religion and helped them to progress" through the belief still "that everything good that has happened to the black man has been thanks to the white man's generosity," and on to the authentically good things that in fact the Church has done. The white illusion that "we know best" is so profoundly engrained that even when black priests point out the contradictions which so afflict black men, they appear not to be taken seriously. I have seen letters in which some are reprimanded for "insolence" and for "daring to question" their bishops. As Father August Thompson, a member of the Black Priests Caucus, remarked when he was chided by white religious colleagues for "stepping out of line" by telling the truth too bluntly: "Blessed are the peacemakers, for they will catch it from all sides."

Part of the disillusion has come from white leadership's inability to disabuse itself of this "we know best" syndrome. Many of us have gone on and on talking with white religious and civic leaders over the years, analyzing the difficulties that could lead to fratricide, and being dismissed as "unduly pessimistic"—sometimes only a few weeks before their community exploded. After their community exploded, their old "we know best" syndrome remained intact because they simply refused to see the true causes and began to look for the Communists and "traveling black agitators who came in and stirred up our good Negroes." Sadly enough, such men really believed that the explosions had come from outside causes. Black people, knowing intimately the situation that causes such explosions, are plunged into profound disgust at the suggestion that some outside Communist or black agitator had come in to tell them that they were in an unhappy situation. They cannot believe that white leaders really believe this and feel that it is just another case of the white man finding a scapegoat for his own communities deficiencies.

In the *Report of the National Advisory Commission on Civil Disorders* (1968), the Kerner Commission spoke of the problem as one of "white racism" and were ignored, and massively. Devout Christians complained that the report "blamed everyone but the rioters," which is rather like suggesting that we should blame the powder keg for exploding when the match was tossed. All of this has led to a kind of *a priori* distrust fatal to any real dialogue. These attitudes are widely known in the black community. Churches and educational institutions issue splendid statements, but society still maintains an almost permissive indifference to the crimes of white racists. On the other hand, white society is fervent in its demands that black men be brought to justice. This kind of duality has long since brought black men to despair of a cure for white racism.

This is part of what black men call "the System"—in this sense, defined as that whole complex of customs and traditions that have been passed down in their abusive as well as their good aspects, and that have all the strength of law, plus discriminatory ordinances on the local level. The System has always told black men that they are citizens and as such they should pay their taxes and defend their country from its enemies. That part of it is splendid. However, suppressed minorities have learned to wait, when white society says a good thing about them, because this is too often followed by a qualifying term like the word "but" after which white society says what it really thinks. So, what the System really says to black men is that they are citizens but they should *not* vote in some areas; that they should *not* have equality of education or employment opportunities; that they should *not* have equal protection under the law; that they should *not* be fully self-determining; that they should *not* have equal access to those culturally enriching elements that allow the human personality to expand and become fully functioning—concerts, theaters, schools, libraries, churches. This list of *buts* could go on and on. It differs in its details in different locales. In some areas of the South, black people still find reprisals if they attempt to register to vote. In other areas where no one would think of denying this right, there is the denial of the right to own property, to make housing or business loans. The very courts of justice which should be free of this duality still discriminate in a harsh and paternalistic manner. Bail bonds for black arrestees tend to be higher than those for whites on the same kind of charge. Black litigants in civil cases often receive substantially lesser verdicts while in criminal cases they receive harsher sentences. In any event, the System, no matter what its local characteristics, refers to this whole set of contradictions faced by black men in a white society where norms are established by middle-class whites. White society would find it intolerable to be ruled by an ethnic group other than itself. Black society finds it equally intolerable. The System not only makes no sense to black men, it is deeply persecuting and frustrating precisely because white America imposes the set without perceiving what it is doing, without *experiencing* what its effects can be.

The white church, without desiring it or intending it, is part of the white society that imposes the system—or at least that has not understood how to clarify and rebut it effectively. The black man can judge only by the evidence presented to him. Some of the evidence has been excellent, like the activities of priests, rabbis, activists and writers, who have been curative and encouraging to black people precisely because each sought not merely to "help" black people, but to help all of society in the area of human justice, and because each of them saw the tragedy of the white racist, as well as his victims. "The racist is the greatest challenge the Church faces today in both the North and the South," observed Will Campbell. "One might say that he is the true adolescent of adult Christianity; certainly the Church must not tolerate what he stands for, but it must not abandon him in its attempt to force him to maturity." Churches give the impression that they are "white" rather than human-divine because too often, all in condemning racism and injustice verbally, they do not make clear the distinction between loving the racist and refusing to tolerate what he stands for. Churches, in fact, frequently give black people the impression that they tolerate very well what the racist stands for. This is why black priests, who love the Church, could be driven at last to refer to it as a "white racist institution" after black men in the streets had been calling churches that for a long time.

Another painful truth: Sociological data is drawn from these patterns. Even white scholars study the evidence and, understanding little or nothing of the causes, talk about the instability of family life and the frequency of common-law marriages (as if these were racial or ethnic characteristics), feel strengthened in their prejudices and in their conviction that black people are *intrinsically different.* They then use this as the excuse for perpetuating the very System that has created the damage. This cycle, so obscure to most whites, is intrinsic to the lived experience of blackness.

This is one of the reasons black people resent not only the overt bigot but are learning to resent even more deeply what in the old days were called "good whites"— the good whites, on whom so many black people counted, have not understood in sufficient numbers the core problems of the *intrinsic Other* and the *System* and have, therefore, failed to repudiate them and their deadly effects on the black community. The "good institutions"—schools, hospitals, courts—have not, after all this time, seen deeply enough to come forth with the profound dynamism needed to bring about fundamental change: to cure racism and remove its taint from our highest institutions; to secure justice without any racist modifications; and most basic of all, to repudiate distorted views of what constitutes man in his essence, thereby lifting from black people the psychologically murderous burden of the *intrinsic Other* concept that exists massively as the foundation-stone for the whole structure of racism. We are not yet near such fundamental change. Worse, despite the chaos that causes us such anguish, we appear not yet convinced of the desperate need for such change—for the salvation of all of humanity. We still hear it daily, often from important churchmen, the glib suggestion that if all rights were immediately restored, chaos might result.

We still encounter overwhelming evidence, in the media and in our churches, halls of state and courts, of the prime racist principle: *Blame the victim.* We still find white citizens affronted because, having restored to black citizens a portion of those rights which this country guarantees equally to *all* citizens, black people have not fallen on their knees in gratitude; but, on the contrary, express growing bitterness that we continue, through complicity, silence and fear—to withhold any of them at all.

"White Christianity"

Black priests especially realize how tragic and deep is the black man's distrust: their cry is that we not go on in this terrible waste, that we understand the System and that we correct at profound levels the whole concept of the *intrinsic Other*. "The saga of the Negro and Catholicism," writes Father Jerome LeDoux, "has often been underscored by reversed leadership. Too often it was a lay magazine or lay speaker who cried out for moral wholeness, for charity, for justice. Too often, it was even the secular press dragging a silent clergy in its train. Most dismaying of all, the Church has been a tail light in the very issues in which leadership should justify her very existence. The civil courts have demolished many barriers which the Church by divine obligation should have disposed of long years ago. Can you imagine anything more incongruous than being allowed to eat where you want before being allowed to worship where you want?" Father LeDoux also makes the crucial point that much of the heroism of the advocates of justice simply should not have been necessary. "Happily, the past was not all shadow and bungle. There were the giants like Father John LaFarge, who labored untiringly with pen and the spoken word to arouse the slumbering conscience of a nation. There was also the occasional pastor who went completely out of his way to guarantee a measure of charity and justice to the minorities. Self-sacrificing Josephites, Blessed Sacrament Sisters, Holy Ghost fathers and Cardinal Ritter set the pace which our Savior would have set. The pity is that these relatively few individuals did work created not so much by a lack of laborers as by their neglect. For all the generosity and devotion, their work should have never been necessary. Canon law tells each pastor that he has a grave obligation to care for all the souls in his parish."

A sense of urgency permeates the statements of black priests and nuns. They have seen the tragic waste and have seen that attitudes, though changing, do not change in pace with black people's reality. "Their patience has not just worn thin in these matters," Father LeDoux observes, but "the skin is all gone." It is this time-lapse between white society's perceptions and black society's reality that has become so crucial. Black parents, realizing the damage done to their children, because men simply do not seem to be able to give up or heal their racism, say: "How can they go on asking us to watch our children being ruined just so they can go on indulging their prejudices awhile longer?" Black parents see this as massive fraud committed against them by white societal attitudes. They see it simply as one group of citizens, handicapped by racism, cheating against another group of citizens—nothing less.

Religious organisms like the Black Muslims began to grow rapidly in membership. Young black students in colleges and high schools asked: "Isn't it true that perhaps Christ is for the white man and we blacks must look toward Mohammed, the prophet of Islam?" Our explanation that the damage came not from Christian ideals but from the mutilation of Christian ideals by men who professed Christianity, had little effect. The burns were too deep. Black men did not see that we would come to the light in the near future. Our actions and attitudes as Christians simply indicated that our parochialism as "white Christians" was entrenched to a hopeless degree. During the 1960s, when "white Christianity" was in low repute among black people, I was frequently asked to speak before audiences—whites and blacks, Protestants, Catholics, Jews and Muslims. Often I would speak about men like Benjamin Mays and Martin Luther King, because their Christianity was deep enough and strong enough to produce heroic action and the redemptive effects of unearned suffering. In those years, black Christians demonstrated to the world a determination to save this country through love. Nonviolent resistance—not passive resistance—was the keyword; nonviolent resistance that might "bring about a transformation and change of heart," said Dr. King. Black Christians by the millions responded to a call for what amounted to heroic charity. Nonviolent resistance challenged black people to love their oppressors until those oppressors were cured of the terrible sickness of racism, healed and liberated from the need to oppress others. At the same time it called for implacable resistance to discriminatory injustices. One of the ironies of history will be seen in the fact that nonviolent resistance, based on the principle of passing through the Beatitudes in order to arrive at beatitude, anchored in the redemptive power of unearned suffering—was suspected of being "subversive" and called "communistic" by white Christian racists who were not able to distinguish between a Communist principle and a profoundly and essentially Christian principle.

Black Americans placed hope in an authentic Christian solution. They believed, they marched, they prayed, they sang, they sacrificed, they took the beatings and the spittings and the cattle prods and went on praying for their abusers—those white racists who called themselves Christians and patriots. Any person who opposed their racism could be certain of character-assassination, attempts to impugn one's morality, economic reprisals, rumors. Question-begging epithets—the repeated use of certain terms long enough and loudly enough in the certainty that they would finally make an impression on unreflecting minds—were standard tactics. Due to the duality of views, it is virtually impossible for racists to make their judgments conform to a reality that is also the black man's reality and takes into account the nuances of oppression. Any theology that ends up justifying, for whatever reason, the racist suppression of any person or group is not a Christian theology. Black theologians go even further: To deny the reality of oppression is to deny Christ. Black thinkers simply reject any theological equivocation on this point and call it "the work of the Antichrist." Black people often read white men's "theologizing" about racism, whether liberal or conservative, with justifiably jaundiced eyes.

The criteria of justice are objective, not subjective, and therefore should have nothing to do with a person's political leanings. Justice demands rendering every person their due. To render anyone less than their due, no matter what are the subjective reasons, is simply injustice. Since the objective criteria of justice are not met when modifications are introduced, how can men speak of "moderate justice"?

On Our Doorstep

Very often I will be warmly received by large audiences in the North, but invariably some well-meaning white person comes up after a lecture, offers thanks for clarifying the principles which we call American and then adds, "But of course we have a different situation here." We have become a nation of exceptions to the very principles which we applaud, that we claim to espouse. It is not so much that we do not repudiate the pattern; it is that merely by acquiescing to it, we acquiesce to the racism that is ultimately as destructive of the consenting and dominating group as it is of the victim group. It is this that black people see so clearly, and really cannot understand how we fail to see; namely the immense cost to the whole community when racists dominate it with fear and violence. Inevitably, we have been led to the predictable condition of Mississippi, which has become a police state.

This was so clear when we tried to get information in and out of Mississippi about the killing of the three young civil rights workers. Dick Gregory had been in to do the preliminary information-gathering right after the disappearance of the three young men, and had learned the name of the tip-off man who had telephoned to tell the police to hold these young men for the killers. I wonder how many of us know what happened to James Chaney's mother. Mrs. Chaney knows what happened to her son, every nuance of what happened. She knows that he was picked up by white men who had committed the murder with the police. She knows that they chain-whipped him to the point of death, and then shot him. And still that was not enough. The word went out: See that the mother does not make a living; see that nobody gives her a job. So she was fired from her job in a bakery on the pretext that during her period of intense mourning for her son's martyrdom for trying to protect the rights and liberties of the great American dream, she had missed too many days of work. And she still does not have a job because no one dares hire her for fear of reprisals from the racists.

I recall another visit to Mississippi when I was sitting in the home of a black family. A few weeks previously, their oldest son had failed to come home one night. The police found him dead, sitting behind the wheel of a car. Then, in a voice I hope never to hear again, a voice deadened of any life or hope—the mother told me when they had found her son, he had a great cavity in his chest and, in her words, "So many bullet holes in his head, I couldn't even count them." And the coroner had called it death by heart failure. So the dehumanizing goes on, and the gradual disrespect for human life. Coming out from this experience, I stopped to get a cup of coffee at a road side stand. I saw a young white teenager there, and presently another young white man came in and sat down beside him. And as calmly as though they were speaking of the weather, he said, "Well, we got another spook last night." They sat talking like that about the destruction of another man's life.

We are shocked by these incidents. But what we fail to see is that these are not isolated incidents. And though we look at them as such and suggest how much better things are looking, the black citizens of this country have never been more somber. For what is in the bone and marrow of the black community is not so much the horror of these grotesque atrocities, as the conviction that this is a pattern of action. The bombing of the children in Birmingham was not the first bombing, but the forty-fifth. The killing of the young civil rights workers in Mississippi followed a year in which there were sixty-nine similar atrocities, for which there was not one single arrest! Every one of these incidents is not an accident; it is the inevitable product of generations of racism that goes on unrepudiated. And these patterns of permissive violence and injustice are maintained everywhere that men do not stand up and cry *No!* I have gone into the worst of these areas after crisis situations, and I have begged the black community not to kill back. Many have criticized me for this, arguing that if I did not discourage them from retaliation, and if they struck back a few times, maybe we would see that they are not going to take this kind of thing any longer. Other than the purely human reasons of being sickened by the killing, I beg black people not to strike back because I know that organizations like the Klan and other racist groups are deliberately trying to create a tension of strike-back. They have told me this face to face, and have told others who have infiltrated the Klan, that "if the niggers try just one thing, we're armed and we'd walk shoulder to shoulder through nigger town and kill every man, woman and child just like they were dogs." This is the kind of dynamics with which we are working, the kind of violence we are trying to hold back.

Does this sound like the United States of America? I fear that it does, and most especially during the violent decade of the 1960s.

—1968

A Time To Be Human

I

I do not represent myself as a spokesman for black people or for anyone else.

I will simply talk about my own experiences with racism, both before and after the *Black Like Me* experiment.

Today, in 1977, many believe that racism and prejudice are things of the past in this country, and that civil rights legislation and greater enlightenment have conquered discrimination. It is true that things have changed in the past fifteen years. Blacks and other minority people can eat and find accommodations and most can vote. But it is also clear that racism and prejudice exist everywhere. No country is spared.

In some American cities, tests have been made. A well-dressed black lady with perfect credentials will look for apartments in better-class neighborhoods. Often she will be told every unit is taken, that nothing is available, that those empty apartments have just been rented. An hour later a well-dressed white lady, with essentially the same credentials, will follow in her footsteps and find vacant apartments. Such experiments were reported in *The New York Times* during the 1970s.

Most newspapers do not talk much about such incidents now. Racism is no longer "news" and therefore many live with an illusion that all the problems have been solved and that we enjoy racial harmony. But the minority press does carry full coverage of racial injustices and minority people are aware of the crippling extent of racism in their own lives. As a result we have continued to be two groups of citizens—the black minority and the white majority—with entirely different sets of information.

The deepest shock I experienced as a black man was the realization that *everything* is utterly different when one is a victim of racism. To my mind this country is involved in a profound tragedy. The problems of racism will never be solved until we can learn to communicate with one another. Yet we have never listened to the words of minority spokesman who have told us truths about ourselves and our country.

After my experiment as a black man in the South, part of my work involved going into cities all over this land to set up communications between black and white leaders. Often I found myself in situations where I sat conference tables with blacks and whites who wanted to solve the problems within their local communities. I knew, and every black person seated there knew, that any of them could tell the whites the truth about prejudice and injustice at the local level far better than I possibly could. But because I was white once again, I could tell the truth without antagonizing the whites. If a black person said exactly the same words, no matter how tactfully he or she might put it, white leaders would be offended and the attempt at communication would turn into anger, with whites referring to blacks as arrogant or rude.

Whites always think that such misunderstandings occur somewhere else. They cannot really believe that black people in Wichita, Kansas or Oakland, California felt the same resentments and frustrations as black people in the Deep South. They also cannot believe that they carry prejudices as deep as those of white southerners.

I was once called in to give a talk on racism in a small town in Pennsylvania. The town had no black residents, although a black industrial psychologist held a position there. The problem there, they said, was between Protestants and Catholics. A white professor at one of the local colleges got Protestants and Catholics together to sponsor my lecture. The house was crowded.

I spoke frankly about the way in which people are persuaded they are not prejudiced and who do not want to be prejudiced can be tainted with racism without ever perceiving it. I talked of the difficulty most people have in listening to truths from black people without becoming offended, whereas they would applaud those same truths coming from a white person. In that sea of white faces, I watched the face of the black psychologist. He smiled and gave a slow nod of approval.

Afterward at a reception for those who had helped sponsor the lecture, the white professor was jubilant. He said it was the first time local Protestants and Catholics had got together on any project, and that it had been a glorious success. Turning to the black psychologist, he said, "Don't you view this night as a turning point in our community?"

"Well, I'm not so sure about that," the black man said.

"What do you mean?" the professor asked quickly.

"I mean that I'm the only black man in this community. I have a fine job and am paid a good salary. But so long as I have to house my wife and children in a town twenty miles away because no one in this town will rent or sell us a house, then don't expect me to get excited about your 'turning points,'" the psychologist said calmly.

The professor almost shouted, "Well, I'll tell you one thing. If you have that kind of attitude, I don't know how you can expect us to do anything for you."

The psychologist would not back down. He held to his point, angering more and more whites even though he never raised his voice or spoke rudely. I saw that a crisis was near, that tempers were getting out of hand, and I said, "This is very interesting. When I talked about the same sort of thing earlier this evening, none of you thought it really applied to this community. You thought I was talking about other people in other parts of the country. Now this man is telling you exactly the same truths I discussed earlier. You gave me a standing ovation; you are furious with him for saying the same things."

It was a cold slap. The professor who had been in such a fury saw the point immediately. He apologized for his bad behavior and thanked the psychologist for helping him to see his own prejudice.

So this has always been, and remains, a great problem, even with the sincerest people. Exactly the same thing holds when Native Americans and Chicanos try to make people understand their problems.

II

My first vivid memory in life begins with the word "nigger."

As a small child I used that word in speaking about a black man in my grandfather's grocery store in south Dallas. I had scarcely spoken when I was jolted by a hard slap across my face and by the anger of his voice as he snapped, "They're people — don't you ever let me hear you call them niggers again."

I will write here about the South, not because the South is more racist than any other corner of this land but because that is where I was born, in Texas, and where I had my early formation. Also, the patterns that formed us in prejudice are a little clearer and easier to understand in the South. But basic patterns are the same everywhere, even though they may appear to differ.

Many of us in the South had a formation that built racial prejudice in us and at the same time persuaded us that we were not prejudiced. Often we were taught to look down on the viciously prejudiced, to view them as "white trash." Many of us had the kind of experience that turned us into racists without our ever understanding what was happening to us.

As small children many of us had the experience of frequent and close contact with black people. We were allowed to play quite freely with black children. We were often reared with the help of a black lady. You did not have to be rich to have black help in those days. Our early years were often surrounded by the love of black people. But when we were still very young, perhaps six or seven, society, in the kind and gentle voices of our parents and other elders, did a terrible thing to us.

Society told us that the time had come when we must stop playing with black children. We were made to understand that we had to change, in subtle ways, our attitudes toward the black lady who helped care for us. I remember my Georgia grandmother, for example, telling me that I was getting too big to sit on that black lady's lap.

Society explained to us that black people preferred it that way, that it would embarrass them if we did not change our behavior and draw away. These explanations, filled with racist myths, led us to conclude that black people were somehow "different" from us in their human needs and desires, that they were not frustrated by things that would frustrate us.

So we were allowed to learn to love black people and then we were taught in a sense to stop loving them. But this was done so gently that we grew up with the illusion that we continued to love those whom we patronizingly called "our Negroes." We saw them as "different"—we viewed them as *Other* and always that implied that they were somehow inferior to us. Yet our distress over cruelties blacks suffered at the hands of whites only strengthened our belief that we were not prejudiced.

I recall an incident when I was seven. Whites lynched a black man in a town ninety miles from where we lived. This lynching was given wide publicity. They even postponed it for three days to bring in special tourist trains for people who wanted to see it. Two thousand tourists—men, women and children—flocked into that town of Waco, Texas. According to the contemporary newspaper accounts, the lynching took the form of burning the young man at the stake. Parents held their children above the crowd so they could see what was going on. But great numbers did not go. We sat at home, hearing our parents cry in anguish against such monstrousness. How could "civilized people" in this century burn a fellow human being at the stake? How could parents take children to view that horror? A few days later we watched our parents' sadness when it was revealed the mob had lynched an innocent man. Such incidents persuaded many of us that we were not "like that." We detested the "white trash" who did such things. We detested their racism, and this led us to believe that we had no prejudice.

All of these early learned behavior patterns went deep in us. In denying our own prejudices, we still thought racism was "human nature," which it is not at all. What we failed to realize is simply this: when children are formed in an atmosphere that permits the suppression of fellow human beings, it ends up tainting us in ways we never dream. Surely few crimes are more tragic than the crime of fostering in children a false view of what man is by teaching them to believe that any other humans are basically different in their human needs.

Similar patterns hold true everywhere. In Nazi Germany non-Jewish children were brought up to view Jewish people as *Other*. And once we believe that a group is "different" then we can believe they do not deserve the same rights and liberties we always claim for ourselves. Many of us go through life without realizing how deeply tainted we are by these prejudices. When we do realize it, someone has usually had to point it out to us.

Such an event occurred to me when I was sent to school in France in my teens. I attended a *lycée* where we had a few black students. As a person who thought himself without prejudice, I was delighted to have black people in my classes. It was the first time I had ever experienced such a thing. And yet the first time I went out to a public eating place with a fellow student, when one of those same black schoolmates I had been so pleased to have in class came in and took a table across the room, I reacted according to the old patterns I had learned. I pushed my chair back from the table and asked in an offended voice: "Do you allow *them* to eat in the same restaurant with us?"

"Why not?" my French schoolmate asked bluntly.

Why not? I realized with a sick feeling that I had grown into my teens without ever hearing anyone ask that question. Worse, I felt astonished that I had never even thought to ask it myself. I had simply accepted the "customs" of my region which said that black people could not eat in the same room with us. Why couldn't they? It had never occurred to me to ask. Only then did I realize how deeply I was prejudiced, and how it formed my thinking about other human beings. Still, if anyone had suggested we practiced racism I would have denied it with all my heart.

During those years in France I witnessed the rise of Hitler. I thought racism concerned only the Nazi suppression of Jewish people, and because the victims were Jews I made no connection between what murdered them in Europe and what afflicted minority people in America. I heard the Nazis say the same things about Jews that I had grown up hearing about Negroes, but didn't recognize the similarities.

III

When World War II came, in 1939, all Americans were ordered to return home. Since France was a country that helped to form me, I could not see deserting my friends there in this time of great trouble. I remained in Tours and soon became involved in the underground and resistance movements.

In those early days of the war, most of our efforts were concentrated on saving Jews from the Nazis. Teams smuggled Jewish families across the border into France and turned them over to other teams who guided them to the city of Tours. There we hid them in cheap boarding houses until we could arrange transportation to take them to the port of St. Nazaire where other teams took them to England.

We had some success at the outset. But when Nazi armies began to invade France, government regulations required we carry identification and safe-conduct papers. These papers were checked every two or three blocks. In those early days, we were unskilled. We had no way of getting papers for the families we were hiding and could not get them to safety.

One night an event occurred that gave me my first clear insight into the basic reality of racism. That night I had the terrible task of going into those rooms in boarding-houses where we had hidden our Jewish guests to tell them we were not going to succeed. We had moved them that far toward freedom, but the German armies were catching up with us and we had no way to move them any further. When I went into those rooms that night the parents guessed why I had come even before I spoke. They said they knew it was over for them, that as soon as the Nazis moved in they would be rounded up and shipped to concentration camps. Then they did something that shocked me. They asked me to take their children away form them, because we could move children under the age of fifteen without any papers.

I realized then that I was in the presence of terrible human tragedy—the tragedy of parents who love their children, who had little hope that they would ever see them again, who were giving their children away to a virtual stranger so that at least they would escape the concentration camps and the gas chambers. The full force of this tragedy was there in all its reality in those rooms. Suddenly all our endless conversations as university students seemed empty and meaningless. Racism, with the rise of Hitler, had been an obsessive topic of conversation among students, the great intellectual preoccupation. But sitting in those rooms with men and women and children, innocent of any crime, pursued only because they were born Jewish, made me realize that we had never understood anything about the true evils of a racist system that solved problems by murdering those men, women and children.

Everything became clear: the smallness of those cheap rooms, the brightly flowered wallpaper, the living, breathing human beings whose lives no one would now be able to save. And I knew then that I could walk out into the street and meet people who considered themselves perfectly decent, who had no knowledge of what was going on inside those rooms and who would go on rationalizing and justifying the very racism that had led to the tragedy in those rooms.

Sometimes in discussing racism with people, I wish I could simply take them into such rooms in this country. I think of the rooms where I have sat with heartbroken human beings who happen to be black and who have suffered great tragedy for no other reason. I think of a room in a farmhouse near Hattiesburg, Mississippi, where I sat with Mrs. Leonia Smith, the mother of Clyde Kennard. Looking into the grief-stricken face of a mother whose son had suffered martyrdom, I knew that the scene was no different from the scenes in those rooms in France and that the same conditions held. I could go outside of that room and find people who considered themselves decent human beings, and who—knowing nothing of the reality within that room—went right on rationalizing and justifying the racism that led directly to that tragedy within that room.

The list of rooms could go on and on, and they are not only rooms in the South. Similar scenes occur in the ghettos of every major city in this land. I think, for example, of rooms in the ghetto of East St. Louis where I have sat and listened to the despair of parents who say, "What can we do? We can't keep the children locked up in these two or three rooms. But the good influence we try to have on our children is wiped out the moment we let them go and play in an area where six thousand people are crammed together in conditions of poverty, anger and despair."

No, racists have not lynched or shot or beaten these young people to death. But racism has fostered the System that every day murders them psychologically, intellectually, spiritually. Black people everywhere, even those who have not suffered what Mrs. Leonia Smith has suffered, know about such things. The black press has carried this information so often ignored by the white press. Whites who never go inside these rooms always view it from the "outside" and wonder why black people feel such deep rage. We whites have no idea what racism really does to people.

When I returned to the States after World War II, in 1945, I lived in Texas. There I began to hear the racist rationalizations I had heard all my life, but now they took on an ominously familiar sound. How often we heard about "our race problem" and "our Negro problem," just as the Nazis had talked about their "Jewish problem."

It is clear that these are not problems of race, but problems of racism.

A first principle of racism is that you "blame the victim." In Nazi Germany, Jewish people were blamed for everything that was wrong with the country, even their own holocaust.

The same holds true here. Whether knowingly or through ignorance we goad Native Americans into an explosion and then blame the victim. We pile frustration on black people and then blame them for reacting. What suppressed minorities the world over have learned is that racism directed against them has little or nothing to do with what they do or fail to do, that discrimination against them does not depend on them but on the political and economic climate as a whole. So, if we can say, as we do, that no one in this country intends for racism to lead to genocide, the effects of racism are genocidal, regardless of our intentions.

Since we had seen where racism led in Europe, I began to do studies dealing with the problems of racism, regardless of who the victim group might be. One of the striking realizations that came from such studies was simply this: the patterns of racism are identical regardless of where or when they occur and regardless of who victimizes whom. Prejudice always involves an injustice committed by one group against another group for reasons of race, ethnicity, religion or political ideology. It is fatal in the end because it always works to damage *both* groups. Such a realization is immensely important because we are finding people everywhere who do not want to be prejudiced, who argue against all racism, some of whom have dedicated their lives to human justice without ever being liberated from those prejudices. Such people will say the right things and believe what they say, but if they have liberated their intelligence from their prejudices, they often have not liberated their emotions, and will reveal those prejudices to black people at the level of spontaneous responses. Black people encounter this constantly. It is one of the reasons blacks say that "all whites are prejudiced." The statement may not be true, but if you are black it seems to be true.

An important development stemming from this is that many of us equate our prejudices with guilt. And since we cannot admit our guilt, we cannot admit our prejudices, even to ourselves. I tell people troubled by this that there is not necessarily any guilt attached to having the prejudices, since we are no more guilty of acquiring our prejudices than of acquiring a disfiguring mark from some childhood illness. We got both when we were very young and before we could do anything to avoid them.

But prejudice becomes a source of unspeakable guilt when we allow it to cloud our intelligence and to goad us into cooperating with unjust actions. When I was a black man, I asked myself constantly: "Why do people cling to the prejudices that poison them as well as their victims?" These questions are still being asked and they are still valid. What sense does it make to go on perpetuating a System that prevents fellow citizens from becoming fully-contributing members of society? These prejudices spring from early learned behavior patterns that our culture teaches us. Until we see this and learn to break the vicious cycle that it perpetuates, we have little hope for durable solutions.

I have often been asked how it would be if I repeated my experiment today, in 1977, in Boston or Detroit rather than in the Deep South. I have spent years in the ghettos of these and other cities. I know that my life as a black man would be different in some of its externals, but the essential damage and frustration would be the same. I would be just as much the *Other* in those cities today as I was in the South in 1959.

The language would be different, but they would be saying the same things. Instead of saying, "We don't want niggers in our schools," they would be talking in such coded phrases as "forced busing" and "quality education." My educated white colleagues would still be hearing blacks speak in a "dialect" and they would see only those things that reinforced the stereotypes they have always held. The major difference is that today, if I were black, I would no longer be grinning and yessing.

IV

Looking back on the 1959 *Black Like Me* experience nearly 20 years later, there were certain key insights I did not learn until months, even years after.

I had never for one moment thought I would pass as a black man to other black people. I had not even intended to try. I had thought that I would simply explain to black people that I was a white man doing a sociological experiment. It was not important for me to pass to black people. My experiment involved white people and how they would treat me once they saw me as a black man.

The reasons why I thought I could not pass to black people, I realize today, are deeply significant. They have to do with "thinking white." First, I did not think I could possibly pass because, although I had the skin color, I did not have the bone structure or facial conformation or color of eyes that we think of as "Negroid." Yet I did not have to be in the black community, as a black man, for more than an hour to see what I had never before noticed as a white man. I saw black people with every type of bone structure, every type of facial conformation, and every density of pigment from so heavy it was black to so light it could not even be perceived. I saw black people with blue eyes, green eyes, gray eyes.

In a land where white men have abused black women sexually for so many years, the vast majority of black people in this country have white progenitors somewhere in their background. The pure African type is a rarity. Black people are deeply aware of this and, in almost every home in which I was given shelter, blacks discussed quite freely and openly "where the white blood came from."

But whites do not see these realities. We think of blacks as looking a certain way. How often have we heard the expression, "They all look alike to me"? When we look at black people, we see them in stereotype. We now know that a deeply held prejudice will actually cause our senses to accommodate to the prejudice rather than to the reality. Time and time again this has been demonstrated to me in my later experience.

When I lectured at the University of Washington, I was introduced by a black anthropologist with the clearest gray eyes I have ever seen. Since she introduced me, the whole audience saw that she was black and had gray eyes. That night I did not discuss this matter of how the senses will accommodate to a deeply held prejudice rather than to reality. After my lecture I stood on the side of the stage talking with the anthropologist when a white woman asked if I would remove the colored glasses I was wearing. I did so, and she looked into my eyes and asked: "How could you possibly have passed when you don't have black eyes?"

I immediately introduced her to the black anthropologist.

She shook the black lady's hand and looked into those clear gray eyes. But she never caught on, because she turned back and waited for me to answer her question. She had just looked into the gray eyes of that black lady, but she still believed that all black people had black eyes.

That is part of what black people mean about "thinking white."

The second reason I thought I could not possibly pass sprang from the same basic error of stereotyping people. I am embarrassed to admit it, but I did not think I could pass because I did not talk in what we think of as a "Negro dialect," and of course I did not even try. We still have vast numbers of people who think that unless you sound as though you were reading *Uncle Remus* you could not possibly be a black person. I have grown up hearing black people talk and yet it was not until I was black and living among blacks that I came to realize one hears just as many speech patterns among black people as one does among any other group of Americans. This was especially true in those days of rigid segregation when you might have been rubbing shoulders on one side with a black Ph.D. and on the other with someone scarcely able to read. But here again, we go on "thinking white."

We go on proving that a deeply held prejudice will cause our senses to accommodate to that prejudice. White college professors invariably ask: "What did you do about your voice, your dialect?" This is one of the most crucial stumbling blocks in relations between whites and blacks, and the reason why communication is so frustrating. Black people constantly encounter whites, well-meaning and often educated, who simply perceive blacks in a totally unrealistic manner.

This is called *selective inattention* and it means most of us pay attention not to how a black person looks or to how he pronounces his words but only to those things that reinforce the stereotyped caricature we already hold of black people.

So, I discovered immediately that I was going to pass to both whites and blacks, and this presented me with an ethical problem. I could not stay in the homes of black people under false pretenses, so I would try to tell my hosts the truth. I would say, "Before I can accept your shelter and the food from your table, I have to tell you a truth about myself that may surprise you." They would look at me expectantly and then I would announce: "I am not really a black man. I am white."

The looks of pain and distress in the eyes of my hosts told me clearly what they were too courteous to say. Their looks said: "Now I wonder what that preacher is doing saddling us with this black man who *believes* he's white?"

Throughout the *Black Like Me* journey, no one ever believed me except the one man [Sterling Williams] who had known me when I was white. The others all thought I was suffering from some sort of delusion. Their eyes told them I was black and they believed what they saw. Only later when the story received wide publicity did they believe that I had been telling them the truth.

When I began my experiment, I believed like many whites that black people led essentially the same kind of lives we whites know, with certain inconveniences caused by discrimination. But that is only the surface of a much deeper picture. The important thing is what racism does to a person's mind, concepts and whole way of functioning.

My deepest personal shock came with the gradual realization that this was not a matter of "inconvenience" but rather a matter of total change in living. Everything is different. Everything changes.

The first of these great changes occurred when I went out into the community that first morning. As soon as I got into areas where I had contact with white people I realized that I was no longer regarded as a human individual. In our experience as whites, whenever we meet a stranger, an aura of mystery exists between us until the stranger discovers what kind of person we are and until we discover what kind of person that stranger is. When a person is imprisoned in the stereotype others hold of him, that aura of mystery is wiped away.

White society looked at black people, saw the dark pigment, and immediately attributed to them all the characteristics of the stereotype. Whites saw no mystery in it at all. They thought they knew everything about blacks. In their eyes blacks immediately were invested with certain "racial characteristics." White society automatically assumed blacks were indolent, irresponsible, had looser sexual morals, were apathetic, could not be trusted with money, probably had a violent streak; and also that they had a keen sense of humor, a God-given sense of rhythm, a good natural singing voice and a passion for watermelon and fried chicken.

Surely one of the strangest experiences a person can have is suddenly to step out into the streets and find that the entire white society is convinced that individual possesses qualities and characteristics which that person *knows he does not possess*. This is the mind-twisting experience of every black person I know. Here whites will pounce on me and say: "You've never met a black who possesses all those characteristics. I can show you dozens who do." Such whites say it the way they have seen it. I say it the way I have *experienced* it. And I think I can explain why they can say that and why I can say I never met a black person who fit the stereotype insofar as authentic ethnic characteristics are concerned.

White people have always said: "We'll treat blacks right as long as they stay in their place." If you pinned whites down, most could not say what that "place" is, but every black person knows—*that place is squarely in the middle of the stereotype*. Whites created the stereotype to justify their racism and forced black people to act out the stereotype. The same pattern holds true with all racists and all victims of racism everywhere.

Racists say: "Don't tell me I don't know Negroes. Why, I've talked with them about everything under the sun. You can't offend them. They've got no pride. They're all alike." They will go on to ask why, if the stereotype is so untrue, blacks did not repudiate it? The answer is simple. Black people could not repudiate the stereotype because whites would not let them. If they did not play the role, they were branded as "uppity." And every black knew that every day blacks lost jobs, got beaten up, driven out or railroaded into jail for no more than being considered "uppity." The stereotype forced a whole System of behavior on black people, and if they deviated even slightly they were in trouble.

Whites have sometimes argued that I felt this degradation more deeply than black people because it was a new experience, whereas black people had known nothing else all their lives.

This is utterly untrue. It burns anyone, and no person ever gets so accustomed to it that it does not burn.

—1977

PART II

Cathedral of Tours, 1946

Photograph by John Howard Griffin

Poulenc Behind the Mask

In 1954, after the edifying dialogues with my spiritual guide, Monsignor Ernst Langenhorst, I ceased traveling to Fort Worth and returned to a more solitary existence. I was doing very good work on my second novel—uninterrupted, free from worry, and at peace with the world.

I had begun using two recording machines, transferring spoken text from the first, along with the edited changes, to the second. This sped up the process, in that I was spared tedious retypings by working out the problems orally. I used the first machine to edit all the bridge passages and, when that was complete and correct, I transferred it to the second in unbroken sequence. Then a third recording machine was added to the process. The third was used strictly for the tracing of background action, so it would be consistent and followed through, backing up thoughts and dialogue, and forming of itself, if taken out of context, a mute drama.

This was when the actual fascination of *Nuni* entered the picture, this was the element of construction that must give strength and solidity to a novel without ever being made obvious to the reader, like putting on the undercoat of a painting.

It was a brain-crushing job, however, the cataloguing of the specific sensual details of sounds, sights, smells, along with the progression of actions, which had to be made consistent with the general mood of the scene, or in contrast to it.

Those first months of the year, too cold to go out anyway, had been days of intense and unrelenting work, when it seemed as though I had four hands and two typewriters, so rapidly and consistently did I work once the recording machine work had been done.

Ironically, just as I was feeling whole again—both as a writer from the work accomplished in the first half of the year, and as a Catholic due to recovering my faith under Monsignor Langenhorst's guidance—I began receiving letters from Francis Poulenc, the famed French composer. He was experiencing a spiritual and artistic crisis similar to my own, except that he had no Monsignor Langenhorst or someone of his caliber to clarify a crisis or to edify one in his faith. Unfortunately for Poulenc, he had chosen the wrong person for help.

In a letter, dated July 10, 1954, he wrote: "My God, you cannot know the anguish. God knows if I shall ever complete *Dialogues des Carmelites* because I am very ill. It is my stomach. Cancer. In spite of my doctors' reassurances that there is nothing wrong with me, I fear that I will never be able to work again. Will you ask the Carmelite Fathers of Dallas to make a novena that I recover my health and that I may be able to glorify God and the blessed martyrs of Compiègne with my music?"

My initial reaction was one of horror about his situation, and one of total incompetence about how I might be able to help him. The letter continued in the same forlorn tone, as if one lost soul were writing to one whom he had not realized was equally lost!

"I am in terrible fear," the letter continued. "Will God take into account my poor efforts—the Mass, the religious motets? Will He at least see them and me kindly, as another bungler, a *jongleur de Notre Dame?* Please locate a good peasant priest to help me. The priests who are considered 'intelligent' exhaust me."

When I had regained my composure, I wrote back, promising him the novenas he had requested, and asking his permission to send a noted Dominican, Father Gerald Vann, to help him. "He is a master of souls," I wrote. "You can put yourself in his hands."

Poulenc wrote back immediately, saying: "Please, no, I feel bludgeoned by the intelligence of Dominicans. A Dominican would make me lose the remnants of my poor faith in five minutes. No, send me a poor, ignorant parish priest—someone who is good and who will not beat me to death with theology."

This strange correspondence had been initiated when the Discalced Carmelite Fathers at Mount Carmel Seminary in Dallas had asked me to inquire about Poulenc's *Dialogue of the Carmelites,* since I had met him in France on several occasions, and because the Carmelites were especially interested in the fate of his religious opera.

Although we had encountered one another at concerts in Paris after the war and also at the Duthoos' chateau — Poulenc had not made this association. He had answered my query as though I were a stranger and, at first, mistook me for a priest. Even after I clarified the fact that I was a Third Order Carmelite, who had been a close friend of the priests and monks at Mount Carmel, he poured out his agony in a way that I am sure he seldom did to anyone face-to-face. In all his letters, he adjured me to strict silence until after his death. The correspondence revealed a Poulenc who did not coincide with his popular image, or even with my personal impression of him.

Everyone knew Poulenc by sight during the prewar years in Tours. He wore an odd green hat at all times, and it was rumored he never removed it, even in the house. We schoolboys would remark with distaste that he was *trés bizarre* but a great pianist, which, of course, excused everything.

After the war, I went back to Tours during the summer of 1946. I was staying in a room in Jacques Duthoo's *Château de Belles Ruries*, where I practiced on an old pedal less Pleyel piano that had been desecrated by the Nazis.

Poulenc was to come for lunch that day.

None of us looked forward to it. He was too cloying, too precious. He hovered about one with an air of solicitude, almost tenderness, like a puppet manipulated by a Cupertino or a Neri. He gave us the sense of being an unfortunate joke that never came off. Poulenc's visits left everyone with an oversweet taste and always an undercurrent of panic, of suspected tragedy under all of this — of some man helplessly trapped behind a mask.

But none of this appeared in his letters. They were straight — the cry of a heart that could no longer waste time with the mask. "All that your Carmelites are doing for me overwhelms me, and I feel unworthy," he wrote in a letter, dated September 10, 1954.

"I don't know if I have told you all the truth about my case. Here it is in a few words. After months of personal sorrows, overwork and voyages, I felt myself gravely ill. The doctors continued to reassure me. I want to believe them but doubts have gnawed at me for days and nights, and still assault me.

"Alas, these doubts concern not only my physical self. The most terrible pain has been to feel my faith fall at the very moment when I have such need of it. Now, miraculously, you and your Carmelites have extended help, and become a source of extraordinary consolation. Tell them that I am constantly aware of their help and that it is a great balm to me. I have begun the orchestration of the first act of *Dialogues*; but I must give my nerves time to gain health before I undertake the second act. I hope Heaven gives me the strength.

"How wonderful it must be to have a faith without fissures. It is true that many saints knew difficult hours—and I am so far from ever being a saint! I hope God will take into account my religious works...." This letter was followed by another from Amsterdam, dated October 11, 1954, in which Poulenc's depression had returned.

"Forgive my silence, but I find myself so unworthy of your letters and your concern that I hardly dare to write you. I am a poor sinner and I am in a state of the blackest neurosis. I can no longer play the piano. I can no longer work. I have such contempt for myself. I came to Holland to give three concerts in the hope a change might help. But the loneliness is so hideous that I cannot stay in my room. I wander over to the hall, seeking contact with any human, talking with strangers. I have truly the impression that I am the Devil's puppet. Only outside of my room can I find any calm. Redouble your prayers for me, I implore you, and may Heaven help me to sleep again, to work again, to forget and to pray. I am two men now, and the composer Poulenc despises with all his strength the too-vulnerable Francis.

"I want so much to finish my *Carmelites*, but how can I find enough peace, how can I sleep? I am ashamed to write you like this, but you and your Carmelites are the only help I have now. Will God ever forgive all of my follies, all my folly? I want so to honor Him again with a music completely purified of these dregs of trickery and cheapness. I have sinned so terribly, but how much I suffer for it. Pray that my soul be saved from eternal fire because my body and heart burn on this earth."

Throughout the winter of 1954-55, a calmer tone entered his letters. He was back at work on his opera.

In April of 1955 he wrote:

"Thanks to the prayers of your Carmelites, my health returns. Alas, during the nightmare, which clung to me for two years, I almost lost the Faith. All my life I counted on religion to help me die well, and when I had this cancer phobia, my prayers turned to dust. I hope that one day the source of Grace will flow again. For the moment, I feel nothing at Mass. I await the *Ite Missa est* the way I used to await the liberating bell of the *lycée*. It is easy for me, the musician, to thank you, the writer and therefore my brother, from the bottom of my heart for having stood by me during these terrible months."

Poulenc's need to write diminished. A mutually understood silence replaced the flow of letters.

Finally, on October 31, 1955, he sent me this brief note: "My opera is finished and will be performed at La Scala in January, 1957. *Deo gratias.*"

The last letter I received from Poulenc, dated August, 1956, read:

"Forgive my long silence. Yes, the opera is done. It will have first performances at Milan in February and Paris in March. They say it is beautiful. I hope that is true. It is terribly earthy—as I see Georges Bernanos' piece terribly human: Pride; Fear. I hope that the last tableau, a great *Salve* for the climb to the scaffold, will throw a breath of the Spirit into the hall. May I, like Blanche, at the moment when one least expects it, again take my place among the faithful." [Poulenc's opera was based on the libretto by the French author, Father Georges Bernanos, author of many books, including *The Diary of a Country Priest*.]

He concluded this brief letter with these haunting lines: "This word 'faithful' is so full of so many meanings, but I cannot fix my thoughts enough to pray. The vagabond over the years of my childhood."

Some months later, one of the Carmelite fathers phoned to say that the NBC Opera was to premiere *Dialogues des Carmelites*. I drove with another priest to the Provincial headquarters in Oklahoma City. Since television sets are not permitted in Carmelite houses, a group of us were given permission to watch the performance in a friend's home. None of us had seen the score of this work or heard any of the music. All were trained musicians, however, and we were deeply involved, both through our contacts with the composer and because the work concerned the martyrdom of Carmelite nuns at Compiègne.

The first act—yes, it was strangely Mozartian—a flamboyant but elegant composition. It excited us but did not move us.

Then came the remarkable second act where the Mozartian felicity suddenly evaporates at the scene of the Mother Superior's death. She gasps with pain, clutching her abdomen. She cries out her doubts. This is the tortured Poulenc of the letters. His own agony transforms the music. Some of his very phrases are in the Mother Superior's mouth. This is the "terribly earthy" portion of which Poulenc had such fears.

We sat transfixed in the darkened room until one of the monks rose and walked quietly into the kitchen for a glass of water—anything to break the unbearable spell that Poulenc had created.

Seldom in art has a creator trusted himself to create so intensely from the depths of his own entrails. Here and in the last act *Salve*, Poulenc had known how to shed his mask.

We heard nothing from Poulenc after that. He no longer needed to write those anguished letters. His music told us where he was going. A few years later, his splendid *Gloria in C* for soprano soloist, chorus and orchestra echoed through the world's concert halls.

But the Poulenc of the public mask, remained on view to the world—the bounder, the fop, the wit, the exquisitely vulgar and jaunty *Français*. He continued to refer to himself as "half-monk, half-bounder," all in hiding the half-monk part even while he wrote music that revealed it for all to hear. But few heard it.

During a telephone conversation with cellist Zara Nelsova, I learned that Francis Poulenc had died in Paris, on January 30, 1963.

The scene from the second act of Poulenc's magnificent and sacred opera, *Dialogues des Carmelites*, immediately absorbed my attention. In it, the Mother Superior dies, writhing in agony, crying her doubts about her faith. Did Poulenc die that way, too? I knew he had already died that way once, because he had written those letters to me about his spiritual struggle. The death scene of the Mother Superior had been a direct translation into music of his own agony.

Later, pianist Jean Casadesus, the son of our great friends Gaby and Robert Casadesus, sat in my studio a few months after Poulenc's death.

"All of Paris' musical world was there for the funeral," Jean said. "You should have seen it. It was grotesque, a farce, but somehow fitting, as though Poulenc himself had designed it for a comic opera. A real *blague*. There were all of those great musical figures. And then a mob of painted and effeminate young men swarmed in. Even his funeral had an air of the ridiculous. It was a typical Poulenc finale," he concluded with a pained laugh.

Haunted still by Poulenc's obsession of pain and suffering, I had associated his death with the earlier death in his opera's second act.

"How did he die?" I asked Jean.

"It was completely unexpected. He just dropped dead. Suddenly. A heart attack."

The funeral might have been a typical Poulenc finale. Yet, it was not the real one. The real finale, his final composition, was performed for the first time recently. A religious work, *Sept répons des ténèbres*, almost shocked by its depth and serenity. In it, for the first time, one finds no hint of the old mask. In it, Poulenc no longer despised whom he called the "too-vulnerable Francis."

Both somehow fused into the music, allowing the composer to succeed in doing what he had so long desired to do: "to honor Him with a music completely purified of those dregs of trickery and cheapness."

—1964

Fraternal Dialogue

July 16, 1964, Huy, Belgium: Have spent the day at Father
Pire's University of Peace—students from all over the world.
Later, I am finally settled in my cell here at La Sarte, the
Dominican priory. This ancient building, constructed in
1834, on top of a hill over-looking the city of Huy, is like the
monasteries I used to know in France—truly poor and simple.
I am occupying the cell of a Father Leonard, who is away on
a trip. It is a small room, large enough only for a desk, cot
and washstand. The ceilings are very high, the walls lined
with books. A single window looks out beyond poplars to the
lights of the village below. No screens, so the room hums with
night bugs. A vast surrounding silence of other cells. In the
corner near the window, a large crock washbowl covers the
washstand; it holds a carafe of wash water. The water faucet
and toilet are at the end of the corridor.

I feel immediately at home here. Everything begins to
relax. Great contentment born long ago (how many years?)
in other cloisters returns this silent night in this ill-lighted cell.
Occasionally, I hear a footstep. Father Pire never sleeps, so they
say. He moves about his cell across the hall. One of the world's
great men, Nobel Peace Prize winner, Doctor of Theology,
lawyer—36 years he has lived in this building, in a cell like this.

Am torn with the desire to write—to write all of this that is
so new and yet so deeply familiar from my past. And at the same
time, torn to be still, silent—to allow the experience of simply
being here to fill those crusted and calloused places of myself.
Great fatigue overwhelms me, comfortable, even pleasant now
in this quiet, this poverty, this simplicity.

I bought a bottle of powdered Nescafe, and take a long
time preparing some in a glass of cold water. There is time
here—a sudden luxury. Odd, if I had these accommodations in
a hotel, I would be depressed and wretched; as I was when I was
a Negro and could get nothing better. I told Father Pire tonight:
"This seems a planet away from Mississippi."

It is warm tonight, still. Through the open window from somewhere far in the distance below I can distinctly hear an infant squalling. Universal sound, thrice familiar to the heart of any father, familiar to all the nights of men.

All of these hundreds of volumes, many of the large paperbound kind of years ago, yellowed. Some mind inhabiting this cell has read them, pressed their knowledge into his own wisdom. Books in Latin, French, English, German.

July 17: All day at the University. Very good sessions and tonight a most enjoyable concert by a young Belgian pianist, Patrick Grommelynck, student of Vladimir Ashkenase — most gifted. Works by Beethoven, Chopin, Bach, Prokofiev.

July 18: Returned here to the monastery this afternoon to take some photos and do my washing. But there is a water shortage and I was able to wash only one undershirt before the water went off. Very hot and still at six in the evening, but overcast, rain predicted for tonight. Vesper bells ring now in the distance and bees hum in this cell. Darkness does not come until after nine. Covered with sweat in my shirtsleeves. Electricity in the air. Rain will surely come and bring some coolness. I run now — or hobble rapidly — to Vespers in the Chapel

After Vespers, supper in the refectory. Even though I learned to eat fast long ago at the Benedictine monastery of Solesmes, I could not keep the pace. I still had a large portion of bread to consume when I noticed the Prior reach for his bell. He waited, watching me. I crammed the bread into my mouth and he rang. I almost choked on it while we stood and chanted the after-dinner prayers. In the midst of supper the skies turned green, the wind suddenly rose, the refectory filled with a garish glow of lightning. The rain brought a blessed coolness.

The window of my cell is surrounded with some type of large-leafed ivy. Rain rattles against the leaves, so near and clear it is as though it were striking my very eardrums. In the obscurity of the storm, the whitewashed corridors are dark except for the faint light that penetrates from side windows — a beautiful kind of visual repose. Now the wind and rain subside.

Thunder rumbles away toward the distant hills. Two monks converse in loud whispers down the corridor. A door squeaks on its hinges, closing. Silence.

Earlier today the principal speaker at the University was Father Cornelis, O.P. Marvelously clear exposition of the theory of the Fraternal Dialogue. Father Pire is careful that the University of Peace not appear sectarian in any way, but a University belonging to all, welcoming those of all colors and politics and faiths (or no faith). Students from all countries meet, and with no hint of any particular religious or political orientation, learn to dialogue while studying the great problems of our times from medical men, lawyers, philosophers, etc. The accents are on justice and peace—the problems that stand in the way of justice and peace.

More and more I am persuaded that we desperately need such a University in the United States, where great numbers of students could come to learn the techniques of the dialogue and the impediments that prevent dialogue. Odd, I am called to Europe to help teach the Fraternal Dialogue, and yet I have never even been asked to speak about dialogue in all of the hundreds of lectures I give in the United States.

Later, the wind has stopped. A soft rain falls steadily now. From my window a view of gray sky, black poplars, and shinning through their leaves and through the gray mists, lights from the village below. They resemble an upside-down galaxy of stars. The grays of the valley are the same as the grays of the sky at this hour.

July 19: Overcast sky and a chill breeze at dawn. Mass at seven in the Chapel downstairs. Birdsongs and stillness. Green trees and distant hills seen through the haze. Nerves gradually come to a profound quiet. I feel almost stunned by this healing process and sit dumbly while the curative forces of peace and security work within me. A kind of muted harmony settles like mist over the clash and blare of this past year.

Nature is fully in it—the trees, the body—the washings and shavings and feedings and sleeps. The soul rests in these things now in an almost somnolent state, abiding, not counting the time, not concentrating but merely being. A kind of felicity is glimpsed occasionally. The clangor of church bells resounds with clarity through the hazes of this morning near and far.

July 22: Three days of intense work. Press conferences, radio and TV shows, two lectures. Returned here with Father Pire, both of us too exhausted to speak; but we discussed again the need for a branch of the University in America.

I do not understand how Father Pire keeps from collapsing. Since the day of the Hungarian revolt six years ago he has suffered a relentless insomnia. He sleeps one or two hours a night. Sometimes he goes for days without lying down. Whenever I go to the bathroom at night, I often see the light under his door. My admiration for him grows each day. For many years he was a renowned teacher of theology until he began his "works" and, as he says, "abandoned the theory for the practice." But he is so unassuming and so open one has to remind oneself who he really is, and how man thousands of lives he has saved from despair.

I have heard that he reads detective novels to help pass the sleepless nights, to divert his mind from his work. I am reminded of Madam Alexander Grunelius' remark to me of Jacques Maritain's penchant for reading detective novels to distract his mind long enough to allow him to sleep. This lady, whose chateau in Kolbsheim is a resting place, a retreat for the world's great intellectuals, said she was amazed at how many supremely gifted thinkers read mysteries for the same reason. "But they must be poorly written," she explained. "If they are well-written they hold the reader and prevent the sleep." At four in the afternoon, I receive my first mail here. What a joy to hear from daughter, Susie. A nice long letter written in different colored inks.

Day of silence and solitude. Profound sense of peace and contentment here. But there is a change in me due to the years. The fragrance of old incense permeating stones of the Chapel would once have opened up a flood of reactions. Today it merely adds its part to the calm felicity of the senses. I have rested, written letters, walked about the grounds and photographed. For the first time since my arrival there is no physical pain. The skies are overcast but the light, though soft, is brilliant.

I glance up from this page to see my small Leitz table tripod with its rotating ball head—am struck by the beauty of this flawlessly crafted instrument.

My body calls attention to itself by its lack of pain, by the wonder of this new sense of its well-being. This must be the way most people feel most of the time.

July 26: Busy but good day. Trip to Liege in Belgium to see the famous baptismal font in the Eglise Saint-Bartholemy. The church dates originally from the 11th century (1010-1015) and the brass baptismal font, one of the world's supreme masterpieces, dates from 1107-1108. The sculptor is unknown, but believed to be Renier, a goldsmith (or silversmith) who died in 1150. In any case, it was a person from Liege. Impossible to describe the marvelous effect of all elements combining into a harmony that leaves me stunned. Back now after photographing a splendid Chateau-Farm (12th or 13th century) near Madove.

July 28-29, at Chateau de Kolbsheim, Bas Rhin, France: Nearby, the clock at the church rings midnight. I arrived here yesterday to spend three days with Jacques Maritain. Madame Grunelius met me at the station in Strasbourg, Jacques looking skeletal but chipper. The car would not start, however, so while Madame Grunelius went in search of help, the Alsatian attendant at the parking lot came over and asked us to help him push the car out of the way. I protested that Jacques should not.

The attendant said, "All right, grandpaw, remain here."

Jacques replied, "Grandpaw'll remain here then."

But the outing was too much and Jacques was fainting by supper. He had bought some books, shopped and taken me to a café in town for coffee. He retired immediately after supper. I talked with the Grunelius family until ten last night, then slept until ten this morning.

Visited with Jacques around noon, then took a long walk in these splendid gardens, photographed him and the gardens. He told me of the great care Alexander Grunelius takes with these gardens—known as the "philosophers' walk." Grunelius considers it the "vocation of the house" to create an atmosphere of calm—a contemplative atmosphere—for Jacques and other world-famed artists and thinkers who come here (and have for years).

We had a good and pleasant lunch. I photographed more in the afternoon—particularly Raïssa Maritain's grave, as Jacques requested. Jacques then showed me the room where they have arranged the furniture and art objects that Raïssa loved best—many photographs of their friends, paintings and drawings by Rouault, Chagall and Picasso. Jacques asked me to photograph this room and the objects in it, including the artworks by great masters who were friends of the Maritains.

Then, at my insistence that he let me help him, we worked until supper time on the photographs he wants to include in his *Memoirs*. Immediately after supper he went to bed. I visited again with the Gruneliuses. We talked much of Victor Hammer, who helped build and decorate the private chapel here at the chateau, and is a close friend of Jacques, the Gruneliuses and Thomas Merton. I had met Hammer while visiting Merton at the Abbey of Gethsemani. Hammer had designed and printed some of Merton's limited editions and the chateau had copies of all of them.

I told them about Merton sending the Hammer edition of *Hagia Sophia* to my friend, Clyde Kennard, and how it had softened his death. Reluctantly cut short this interesting session to return here to my room at about nine that night to work on the photos for Jacques' book.

Am quite amazed to see Jacques' good spirits, his delight in things, the sharpness of his wit. We are having a thoroughly good time together. The awful anguish over Raïssa's death has finally turned into something no less preoccupying but now peaceful.

July 30: Returned finally this evening from Kolbsheim. Good to be back in this cell again. Father Pire is not back yet from the University, so I went to the refectory, found sardines, boiled potatoes, bread and mayonnaise left over from supper. I ate well. When I opened the door, returning to this cell, an odor of strong French tobacco struck me. I smoke so much the room is permeated with the odor.

At Strasbourg yesterday, the Trans-Europe Express was crowded so they refused to take me since I had not made a reservation. I made one immediately for today—spent yesterday evening photographing Strasbourg—a beautiful city. I ate too much because the food was so delicious.

Walked miles over Strasbourg and now my legs ache. But I walked surprisingly well. I never dreamed my legs would hold up for such distances. But it was mostly flat—little uphill walking at all. Here at Huy everything is up and down.

After an immense dinner last night, I sat on a bench at one of the *quais* under the trees and listened to the water for an hour. Young couples, their arms about one another's waists, passed occasionally, their voices soft and delightful as the summer night air. Listening to them, I felt old—or rather I felt what it is not to feel young. I sat there tired from the afternoon's walk, contented from the supper, and envied them not at all. For a moment this unsettled me, but I realized that if Elizabeth were here it would be different—we would be doing as they. Only we would not have to leave one another at the end of the evening—we would go right on to bed together. When one is young, one is self priming; older, it takes a lot of elements steeped in nature and in the nature of marriage to accomplish the same priming. Much better.

August 1: It has turned almost cold tonight—about fifty degrees. Light rain splatters against the vines that grow around the window. Long and hard day's work. Opening of the new session at the University. Father Pire gave a brilliant analysis of the Fraternal Dialogue, in great depth and the simplicity that finally comes out of complexity. I jotted down some of his statements.

"To speak first without listening is not dialogue, but monologue."

"We must distinguish true dialogue between two from mere double monologue."

"Unilateral declarations published at the same time are simply double monologues. The greatest error is to make people believe that a double monologue is a true dialogue. Monologue separates. Dialogue unites."

"To build brides across chasms that separate us—dialogue."

"Those who oppose dialogue are fanatics. They want only to hear their own monologue, and will listen to no other truth than the one they think they possess."

"Dialogue—to open oneself to the *Other*."

"Dialogue—to escape the prison of words and prejudiced ideas."

"Dialogue—the spirit of honest disagreement."

"The problem of contradictions—the human cacophony."

August 2: Next Sunday I will be in Texas, a continent away. Here at six this evening, a cold sunlight streams through the window of my cell. It casts a magnificent glow into every corner of these white plaster walls. Church bells from the valley float up faintly to us—the sounds of sunset. Otherwise, a profound hush is softened only by hints of conversations somewhere in the valley and a breeze rustling the trees outside. Moments of profound peace. Soon supper, then Matins and Lauds and then I am scheduled to lecture to the monks here at La Sarte.

But everything fades as awareness concentrates on the peace that overwhelms me after the relentless tensions of the past years. It stupefies me. I feel a tremendous pull toward sleep always. I do not resist it, two hour nap this afternoon, waking from time to time to glance out at the sky and the poplars framed by the window, sensing the benevolence of this place and falling effortlessly to sleep again. At four, coffee and a large slice of bread and a banana, alone in the refectory.

My last Sunday here. I'll return surely, but not again to this cell, not again in this cloister because next time I'll bring my family. God willing, and that will be better but never again the same. So I look at everything with the eyes of a last time, feel everything with that special sensibility. And my heart looks ahead to the joy of being with my family next Sunday— but with the dread of the telephone calls, the constant running in the paths of man's inhumanity to man.

Long, long twilights here, almost three hours each evening. In spite of the long sleep and the hours of catching up on rest, one works here; finally much gets done and without great effort. Everything is perfectly organized to let work flow on its own rhythm, naturally, without force or strain.

August 4, the Feast of St. Dominic: The monastery bustles this morning and last night with preparations for the great Dominican feast. The usual profound quiet is hardly less silent, but with movement as everything is cleaned and polished. Young monks carry tables to the refectory, others carry great stacks of borrowed dishes lent for the occasion. A hazy, almost sunlit morning — an air of marvelous festivity.

There is a crowd at Mass. I entered late, but in time to hear the jubilant Frescobaldi trumpeted out on the organ. Strange — sixteen measures of this music, and I felt all that is in me catch the spirit of the day — almost as a shock to the system — a great joy and suddenly I am in the midst of the preparations for dinner. I go to photograph the proceedings now.

Radio, television and press conferences all afternoon. I returned here this evening to dress for tonight's concert — a recital by Jacques Genty and Lola Bobesco, sonatas by Bach, Mozart and Beethoven, performed by two supreme artists. A moving matter — the students dress informally for all of the lectures, no matter how distinguished the lecturer; but they invariably dress for the music with which Father Pire surrounds us, as an homage to art.

While I was here bathing — in two quarts of cold water in a washbowl — three young men from Father Pire's home for refugee children called at the little reception room downstairs. When I went down, they asked me for a conference. One, orphaned when his parents were sent to a concentration camp, told me that war was declared today between the United States and the Viet Cong. I wait alone now for further news with a great weight in my chest. Listened to the news on a transistor radio. No war yet. United States accused of brinkmanship in Vietnam to distract attention from growing racial rises in America. Trouble in New Jersey and Philadelphia. Announced also the discovery of the mutilated bodies of three students—Andrew Goodman, James Chaney, Michael Schwerner—missing in Mississippi.

This is the reality. One speaks of men like Father Dominique Georges Pire as though they were dreamers, when nothing could be less true, if this implies a lack of reality. Father Pire lived through the nightmare of occupation in a village where for each German slain, fifty local family-fathers were shot as hostages.

The same racism, different version, comes to light in Mississippi with the finding of the bodies. The report says James Chaney, the Negro student, was severely beaten before being shot. Dehumanization of the racists.

This is what I go back to, back to the rooms where I must look into the ravaged faces of James Chaney's mother, or Clyde Kennard's mother—and how many mothers of martyrs before we learn to stop justifying our cheating?

—1964

The Little Brothers

I

In my early years in France, I was greatly influenced by Charles de Foucauld who had the extraordinary vocation of going out among non-Christians to lead a life of perfect love, without ever attempting to make a convert, without any proselytizing whatsoever, without doing anything, in fact, except simply living the Gospel and loving perfectly.

Father Foucauld had hoped to pass on his ideas in the form of a new Order. But the life was so severe and so unattractive that during his entire lifetime he never succeeded in attracting a single disciple or follower. There had been other difficult vocations, such as the desert fathers, but none quite like that of Father Foucauld.

Charles de Foucauld was one of the world's extraordinary men. He was an army officer and a count. As an officer, he had taken up a totally bacchanalian existence to such an extent, that in the face of scandal he was forced to resign his commission. His career had taken him to Africa, and upon returning to France he met an unusual priest, an Abbé Huvelin. It was just one of those inexplicable things. Father Foucauld had never entertained the idea of becoming a priest. In fact, he had renounced the religion of his childhood in favor of complete sensuality. But through Abbé Huvelin he developed an interest in religion and finally became a Trappist monk.

Upon entering the Order he was sent to one of the poorest Trappist monasteries, Our Lady of the Snows, and two years later, upon his request, he was transferred to a still poorer one in Northern Syria. After remaining a Trappist for seven years he found that his soul was still unsatisfied, and he was released from his vows.

What Father Foucauld came to realize was that a life in God that equivocates, that is less than total, absolute, and heroic is simply not enough. What he desired was to go into the deserts of the world, the most desolate and barren of all habitable places, where men have been crucified and defeated, and to take work, all the while revealing no visible sign of his vocation. He would live in poverty, according to his conscience.

Foucauld's concept of poverty was absolute poverty: a roof, a minimum of food, and any kind of clothes available. Whatever he had left over he would anonymously and unobtrusively give to anyone in need, and always without drawing any attention for what he had done. Again, it was the idea of living the Gospel perfectly. His life was one of prayer and meditation for those who did not even know about such things. He simply hoped (or perhaps inwardly knew) that resonances from that kind of life had to go out to clean the spiritual cesspools of humanity. What all this really amounts to is the perfect development of charity within the human soul.

Father Foucauld began to practice his philosophy at Béni-Àbbes, an oasis in the Sahara located near Morocco. He was convinced that one day he would have a fraternity of Little Brothers to join him, but these never appeared.

Finally, in desperation, he moved further south to the village of Tamanrasset where he settled down. On December 1, 1916, he let himself be dragged from his hut and without a word of protest knelt while a Touareg shot him through the head.

It is not a difficult matter to understand why Little Brothers never flocked to Morocco and Charles de Foucauld, for his vocation was one stripped of the usual consolations associated with the religious life. The priesthood was not only unnecessary, it was undesirable. There was obviously no need for apologetics if one lived a quiet, sequestered life and sought no converts. Taking the solemn vows of poverty, chastity and obedience was prerequisite to an ascetic life among the most wretched and the most miserable of the earth, without the consolation of an ordered fellowship, or even a priestly fellowship, which one normally associates with the regular monastic life.

This was a practice of monasticism within the world, and there is something quite terrifying about it, particularly if one is to be located either in the Arab countries where Foucauld worked, or in any of the great slums of the world. With great fervor, a young man may throw away his life for a short time, but to think of a whole lifetime of hard work with no single visible result is a fairly terrifying prospect.

II

How then, did the Little Brothers ever materialize? Ironically, they came into existence through the fact that Father Foucauld was like a great many men who seek to be the least known, but who tend to be so extraordinary that they instead become the best known. News of him filtered out of Africa and attracted others into the desert.

Finally, Father René Voillaume headed up an order of the Little Brothers and Sisters of Father Foucauld's, as it was originally called, and which is more popularly known as the Little Brothers and the Little Sisters of Jesus.

The great ferment came after World War II when there were in Europe, as in this country, an unaccountable and unprecedented number of young men seeking entry into contemplative orders such as the Trappists. Some of these men had been closely associated with the internment camps of one sort or another, and I think that they were both privileged and horrified to see unmasked evil. After the awful vacuum left by the War with its Nazism and horror, I suppose men needed to become heroic in their virtue in order to counteract this awful insanity; and so one saw a great number of these young people attracted to this particular vocation.

When the Little Brothers began to organize into a specific entity, the form they selected almost perfectly matched the form suggested by Father Foucauld's ideal. The figures are not readily available, but an amazing number of young people gathered, and of these a great many stuck.

The test was the desert. A novitiate for the men was set up in an absolutely barren spot in the Sahara. They set up tents and lived in silence and solitude with nothing but the sterile landscape and the sky; this was considered the virilizing process. One needed no particular intelligence quotient; one needed only a brief period of training in what the Order meant and stood for.

So they began to go out from the desert. For example, some of the first Little Brothers would go into the slum areas of Marseilles; others traveled with Gypsy bands and never identified themselves. In each case, the Little Brother lived among the needy, not as preacher, but as a fellow.

The system has been considerably expanded since that time. When one is out alone, or at best with another, one needs a more thorough theological preparation in order to cope with the problems that arise, particularly the drying up of the spirit and the constant, incredible, unrelieved contact with human misery and physical degradation. But the initial stage of the program has always been preserved.

The Brothers spend six months in the Sahara to test their vocation. Where there is no distraction, it does not take very long for a man to rely entirely upon his relationship with God, or, if he cannot, to find out that he needs something more in the way of consolation and satisfaction. The men are completely isolated during this period. They sustain themselves on a diet of dried figs and dried dates, or whatever local food is available. Meditation alone must serve as their real sustenance, or they have chosen the wrong profession. Before long they are going to be in places where even the desert rat would appear almost like a friend.

After the Sahara, the Brothers go to one of the houses of formation for three years of theological training. The principal house is located at Toulouse, France. The theology that is taught them is not apologetic; it does not involve itself with the hierarchical structure of the Church. Rather, it is a scientifically precise study of the development of the spiritual life. It is a theology that will prepare one to grow in Christ; unguided, it can be a bewildering experience. It is a theology based upon the precautions of St. John of the Cross.

At last, after having taken the perpetual vows of chastity, poverty, and obedience, the Little Brothers are sent out on their own in areas of the greatest need. They expect no financial support beyond what is necessary to sustain them until they find some work. Many of these men are university graduates and beautifully trained. Under normal circumstances they could command excellent positions, but this is not the point. The point is to find a job that will earn enough for their own poor needs, and if anything remains, it is given away. The type of job is immaterial. If possible, each Brother attends daily Mass, but in any case, he has an hour of meditation every day and says his Office in private. The Little Brother is, therefore, a monk in his own private world.

Theoretically, of course, the Little Brothers do not go out and disappear forever; there is some communication carried on with the house at Toulouse. To the greatest extent possible, Father Voillaume himself is on constant visitations to these young men. But this does not necessarily mean that he gets to them very frequently.

In this way, one keeps the illusion of contact even though it is unlikely that he will ever return to Toulouse. There is no provision that would call one back every certain number of years. Each Little Brother is simply on his own. The beauty of this system is that one does not make decisions in Toulouse for a man who is living with Gypsies, or who works in the slums of some city, since any decision might be grotesque in view of the sort of life he is leading. Therefore, there must be a tremendous amount of ability on the part of the Little Brother himself.

In 1965, the Little Brothers are scattered over the entire world. In America we have two, at least as far as is known — Brother Manual and Brother Roger, who traveled here in 1963. When it became known that they were coming to America, Bishop Wright of Pittsburgh requested that they work in his city. Detroit, on the other hand, was not at all enthusiastic. Typically, they chose to go where they were most needed, which was Detroit. They went very quietly and set about their vocation, naturally remaining separate from the structure of the Church. Brother Roger works as an orderly in a hospital and Brother Manuel works in a pawnshop.

Their vows of poverty are extremely authentic; they live in an old, old house in the ghetto. There they have a tiny chapel where they do meditation, and cubicles just big enough to house their cots and bodies. All of the cell partitions were put up and hand-carved by the Brothers themselves. Each of them also prepares his own meals in a kitchen that looks like somebody else's back porch. While they do not pretend to set up a mission, their doors are always open to anyone caught in an emergency.

Occasionally priests come to visit them, and it is almost as if they come to the Brothers to be edified, and to retreat to the absolutely pure kind of early Christianity where a man acts from no other volition or motive than to act as Christ.

The Little Sisters work precisely the same way, but there are a great many more Little Sisters, who travel to all the slums of the world, never rationalizing themselves out of situations where a Christ-like action is required. It is somewhat difficult for us to imagine them without special garb, intermingled in with the masses of humanity, when we are so used to the traditional concepts of teaching and proselytizing.

III

The story of Jacques Maritain in relation to The Little Brothers is an unusual and interesting one. For years many religious orders had looked upon him and his wife as extraordinary people, and it was an open secret that there was an agreement between Jacques and Raïssa that the one who survived the other would retreat to a religious house. When Raïssa died, everyone held their breath to see where Jacques would decide to go, and what he would do with his remaining years. Since Jacques had a great love of the Benedictines, everyone really expected him to turn in their direction. When he chose to live with the Little Brothers in Toulouse, everyone was quite dumbfounded. Jacques once told me why he selected this Order, and this is a difficult point to make.

To Maritain, they represented the nearest thing to the unspoiled early Christian who existed long ago. And with this kind of Christian there is nothing that one cannot ask. Jacques has been extremely ill, and in another monastery he would have felt himself to be a burden, although nobody else would have considered this so. But at Toulouse, when it has been necessary, he has been taken care of in all simplicity. He is granted solitude, he does his philosophical work, and he is surrounded by a kind of love that is entirely and utterly purified of selfishness. This is where he has survived the terrible blow of the loss of Raïssa.

For a moment, just after World War II, I thought that I had a vocation in the Little Brothers, but having an impediment of blindness at the time, I knew that this was not the case. I was fascinated by the Order, and I was anxious to make clear to the world the heroism of this kind of vocation. I asked for and received permission to go to the Sahara and live their life in order to aid in the preparation of a novel.

As far as I know, I am the only novelist ever given this opportunity. I had the permission, but I never acted upon it.

—1966

The Terrain of Physical Pain

All men know something of physical pain. Great or small, it is part of lived experience. Some men are called to experience suffering deeply and for prolonged periods, to become familiar with its modes and its nuances within themselves. Such men traverse a terrain that goes from the known to the mysterious, each at his own speed of perception.

Science can tell the sufferer much about the causes of pain and some of its effects and perhaps some of its remedies. Each sufferer's inventiveness shows him ways of adapting to his limitations. At first it is hard, concrete. The sufferer comes to know what is known, learns to do what must be done. But soon, with growing experience, these things fade into the area of the mechanical. Then new and vague truths begin to emerge, truths difficult to formulate, and the sufferer perceives that much of what he experiences, much that is most profound in his experience, simply lies beyond the realm of ideas. For this reason speculative explanations of suffering often sound false, off-key to the sufferer because they rarely conform to his own lived reality.

Certainly every sufferer has had the experience of having his condition "explained" to him by people who have had only superficial experience with pain, which is rather like explaining the keyboard to a concert pianist. Nothing is more ironic to the man steeped in physical pain than to be told by the visitor, pink-cheeked with health, that the sufferer is "God's pet," or that God has allowed him "the deep privilege of suffering," even though these things may have some truth in them.

On the other hand, those who have known pain profoundly are the ones most wary of uttering the clichés about suffering. Experience with the mystery takes one beyond the realm of ideas and produces finally a kind of muteness or at least a reticence to express in words the solace that can only be expressed by an attitude of union with the sufferer.

"In these terrible sufferings," Raïssa Maritain wrote in her journals for 1934, "I am able to be sustained somewhat by the processes of tenderness and friendship. Indeed, no fine reasoning could have the same effect. This explains the complaints of Job against his friends who reasoned, however, perfectly well." And she went on to speak of: "This faculty to act at once on two planes—that of concrete experience, demanding and painful, and that of an abstract and liberating conception rooted in the same experience. It has been this for me, and this permits me to live."

In this faculty to act at once on two planes, the French poet went to the heart of the mystery. It is this concept that comes to some sufferers to transform the energies of pain into profoundly creative energies. These may never show themselves in tangible forms, but the intangible effects of creativity are at least as important in the resonances they produce as the tangible ones.

This faculty to act at once on two planes can be dissipated when it becomes merely an attempt to escape an awareness of pain. No, it must be the contrary—an acceptance and an awareness of the reality that exists in pain and that sometimes becomes obsessive in pain, and then a growing ability, from the same root, to stand off and become the observer; and then again, passing on to the observation of other things until at length and in the natural order of things, the observing self comes to the realization that self, even in pain, is less interesting than other objects of contemplation.

It is this realization, which takes time, that ultimately liberates the sufferer: not from his suffering, no; not from an acute awareness of his suffering, no; but from the otherwise exclusive, obsessive, paralyzing, sterilizing enslavement of suffering.

This begins to occur, for example, when the man deprived of some freedom by pain—perhaps the freedom to walk—is initially overwhelmed by the deprivation: absorbed in the deprivation or the pain; then, as he learns, as he lives with it, the interest is less sustained. He can see the person not thus deprived climb steps without any hesitancy and feel some unwholeness because he cannot do that; but then he can begin to see that simple act which to him is now impossible no longer as a reproach to himself, no longer as a reminder of his own deprivation. But in the light of that, from the same root, as a marvelous sight, he sees the man bounding up steps as something extraordinary, beautiful; he sees and marvels at the freedom and lack of pain and concern in the man climbing the steps, and this rather than his own inability is far more interesting. He watches it the way others might watch a great athlete, or a dancer like Nureyev: not in self-loathing because few men are great athletes or have the skills of a Nureyev, but because of the beauty of those who have these gifts.

The sufferer can come to this secret realization: he can view those who do not suffer almost as though they were great artworks, with his own special lights and perceptions, with his own special astonishment. This is not a question really of generosity, but of a deep natural priority of interest. He has begun to perceive that self is less interesting than what is interesting; he has come to learn the difference between what is merely average and what is normal. By the average, he is a deprived and afflicted being, but when this becomes his own normalcy, then the average is simply viewed by him as extraordinary. From this can spring a truth that confuses those who know little of suffering: the core of joy that lies at the heart of even the most intense suffering; the supreme activity of wisdom that does not need movement.

There are few road maps, and there should be few, to guide a man who faces suffering as a new experience. The way ahead is essentially unknown for each sufferer and because of the individuality of each human person the way has to be clarified through his own experience. This can cause great fears at the outset. It can cause a man to play roles, to assume masks of bravery, courage, patience, even when such masks are alien to the reality the suffer experiences within himself. Because he is in unfamiliar territory, the sufferer naturally assumes attitudes he thinks society expects and admires. Before suffering itself can clarify values for him, he begins to search frantically for the reasons for his suffering.

"I suppose God does not let suffering evaporate uselessly," poet Pierre Reverdy wrote in a letter to his friend Stanislas Fumet, "and we can contribute to the good, no matter how incredible that might seem to us, whenever God decides."

Some men grasp this kind of concept as a salvaging one at the outset of prolonged suffering. In searching for "why," men can be driven to accept this as a reason. Men can cling to this concept as an act of faith, can offer up suffering and find some sense in it if "it can contribute to the good." But some men simply cannot. I suspect that to every man who passes into this kind of experience this whole concept, even when it is accepted blindly on faith, is highly dubious, because what is happening to the body, to the rational animal is not really rational: assaults are taking place that the rational mind cannot understand. The mind seeks reasons for what is happening to the body, and so the mind grasps at these "reasons" even while the body casts them into doubt. The body can even lead men to suspect that there are no reasons, that it just happened, that the pain is going to "evaporate uselessly."

Only later, and usually in ways quite different from the expected or hoped-for ones, does the realization come that a transformation has occurred—a massive transformation—the effects of which begin to manifest themselves even while the causes remain obscure; and the man who has suffered deeply can see in these effects that nothing was, in fact, wasted.

Lionel Trilling once observed that culture is a prison unless we know the key that unlocks the door. He had referred to those learned behavior patterns inculcated in men from earliest childhood according to the customs and traditions of culture, patterns so deeply inculcated that men tend to call them "human nature," which they are not at all. Man's individuality has been frequently blunted by the process, which seeks to make men of the same culture resemble one another. The saints have always struggled against this, seeking a reality that transcends cultural limitations and delusions.

One of the things discovered first by those entering into suffering as adults is this contradiction between cultural concepts and the reality that physical pain imposes. Usually this enters the door of humiliation, making such a man aware of his clays, clarifying the tendency to deny (or hide) the animality of his physical self. For in pain, it is the animal self that calls attention.

In a society or culture that has placed great emphasis on "the more or less decent parts" of the body, in which spiritual writers have viewed the body as an impediment, sometimes even the enemy, to spiritual growth, it has been inevitable that men come to delusions about themselves, to want to show God only those more "decent aspects"—in other words, to drift toward angelism where they see as contemptible those things about themselves that the creator obviously saw as good: the animal functioning that is part of man.

The delusion is particularly dangerous because it exists at profound and unconscious levels. It is through this delusion that men still widely believe that man grows spiritually by truncating his humanity rather than by perfecting it. Such men, called to pain, perhaps discover for the first time (and with what a sense of relief) that when man is stretched out in pain before God and before man, in all his nakedness and vulnerability, there are no "more or less decent" parts, and he can become reconciled to that from which he should never have been alienated in the first place. His reality shows him, too, that many of the values he has been taught are blessedly untrue: the idea of strength as a necessary virtue, for example, crashes when a man becomes helpless through physical suffering and has to allow his body to be handled and cared for like that of a child.

The man strapped naked to a table and turned in all directions, even upside down, for a spinal myelitis examination, aware and in initial embarrassment because doctors and nurses are observing him, not only in his nakedness but especially in his very defenselessness, comes to realize that what he has hidden (intellectually, mentally) was not really hidden. It is still there in his suffering body, and finally he has to face it; but simultaneously he has to recognize something far more important: those "strangers" who view his body and handle it, do so in the profound charity of a search for healing. No matter how physically and psychologically painful this may be, he can realize that those who help are lifted to charity through the pain that afflicts his body. For that amount of time, something tremendous and pure has occurred. And he may even feel the deep balm of a first understanding that the body, so denied in some of its aspects, so hated, perhaps, has longed for the same sunlight as the soul; and that in God's sight, if not in man's, there is no blushing, no turning away, no priorities in parts but a reality of the whole.

In another sense, again at levels of pure resonance, once a sufferer can come into intimacy with his suffering, he can come to a deeper perception: the denial of cultural concepts that have led to the belief that fellow human beings if they belong to other cultures, are in fact intrinsically and fundamentally *different*. Pain is universal. In learning this the sufferer finds himself united to universal suffering. Every man who lives, regardless of his cultural or ethnic differences, faces the identical human problems of loving, of suffering, of dying. In the isolation of pain, the sufferer faces these realities and gradually realizes that pain in the body can cure things which are not the body, that it brings clarity to intuitions, unclouds perceptions, and opens up the whole area of intuitive knowledge known as "prephilosophy" that can replace cultural distortions with a reality before which such distortions can no longer stand.

"In the realm of the spirit, it is not so much what we do as what we allow to be done to us," Gerald Vann once wrote. Certainly, at the deepest levels of human creativity, a part of genius has been the ability of men to allow themselves to be used as a sort filter for experience; to accept the experience imposed on them without even judging its value, allowing it to enter, allowing it to teach, and then letting it come back out in some different form of expression—prayer, silence, music, contemplation, art.

Certain masterworks are otherwise unexplainable in human terms: some of the poems of St. John of the Cross, the Mozart *G Minor Quintet*, the great *Opus 132 Quartet* of Beethoven, to mention only a few. In these, experience, often in the form of intense suffering, has been accepted, handled, then released. As Reverdy pointed out, great works tend to happen despite men rather than because of some purely human initiative. "We have to believe that what happens despite us is better than what we do on our own," he wrote.

The sufferer, because he really has no alternative, is forced finally by his suffering to recognize this core truth: things are being done to him. Values he once held are crumbling. Only later, perhaps, will he see that such values are replaced by others. In a society with a mania for organization and a consequent mania for demanding that every action produce a measurable result, he begins to learn that results in themselves are a needless luxury. He may even learn an ultimate wisdom — not to care about results, not to waste time looking for them — submitting himself to the action and allowing the results to take care of themselves, in the knowledge that if "God does not allow suffering to evaporate uselessly," then that suffering is being used and how really does not matter. If suffering does evaporate uselessly, then nothing the sufferer can do is going to change that.

He senses a tremendous liberation from such values. He trusts his humanity which he begins to sense in a personal and individual way. "The world needs results; I don't," he says. Involved in pain, knowing it intimately, he no longer looks on pain as the feared stranger even when it remains in fact the unwanted companion. From his perspective he learns that others fear this unknown, that others suffer in his sufferings, perhaps even more tormentedly because they do not know them with any precision. He learns pity for those who do not suffer but must witness his suffering. The sufferer then takes on the role of consoling those who are spared. When this is achieved, he can offer true solace and can stop being concerned about "playing the brave sufferer."

Very simply then, physical suffering, if the sufferer allows it to do with him what it can — in a kind of simplicity and openness to its teachings — turns the sufferer into giver, into lover, into consoler. Long experience with suffering has taught him that he can bear what he has borne. But he cannot bear it when others suffer. It constantly reawakens him to mercy and to an authentic pity which bring in their wake a melting of the calluses of indifference and unconcern for others. Even the man totally immobilized and locked in pain, *the moment all elements of self-pity have evaporated*, can spread an authentic and curative pity that sometimes seems to blaze from him.

And this is the plane where his paths of experience join the paths of men of the spirit — here he has been driven into the desert, isolated. "A too-great affliction places a human being beneath pity, provokes disgust, horror, and scorn," wrote Simone Weil. No matter how surrounded by men, the sufferer is sometimes isolated, a hermit in the desert of his suffering. Whereas the mystic, the contemplative seeks the desert, the solitude, the essences of reality, the sufferer is taken there by his suffering. Men fear the deserts; men want the security of shelter, of walls, of companionship with people; for who can bear the terrible vastness of too great a view of creation?

The desert, the silence, the solitude — the sufferer is placed there and has to look, has to face the whole of his experience, has to face the infinite. And like the desert dweller, he has to expand with it until it is no longer terror but solace he finds there. He communicates, and more, he can soon realize that even when pain so diffuses his faculties that he cannot utter a single verbal prayer, the pain itself can become the most eloquent of all prayers and he need not preoccupy himself with that. In "allowing it to be done to him," he begins to understand Cassian's statement that there is no perfect prayer if the religious perceives that he is praying. The prayer of pain, the gift of pain.

The sufferer, in his own time, finds himself a great distance from former concepts where he felt he had to offer God and the world something grand, something beautiful and lustrous, something "worthy." He knows now that the great secret is simply not to withhold anything, not to withhold even wretchedness if that is all one has.

There are limits to the joy as well as to the suffering that human beings can bear — so these glimpses into realities beyond the realm of ideas are transitory. However, once experienced, they alter everything from then on. They change the individual. He is no longer average. They become part of the deep originality of the human individual.

These are secret things to the sufferer. If he has entered deeply into this special solitude, he feels words cheapen and distort it. Thus the sufferer sometimes tries to hide his suffering from public gaze, feels uncomfortable when men talk of his "witness," not out of modesty but because men tend to use liberating truths in an arrangement that re-imprisons them in what are merely cultural values. No, these are private things. They become other things when the sufferer is called on to reveal them. We remember the mystic's cry when deprived of solitude by men who wanted his wisdom: "I seek God and you surround me only with religion."

The ultimate and true effects of suffering can only occur, from the sufferer's viewpoint, in the very silence and solitude from which they spring, beyond the realm of ideas. These effects—wisdom, giving, mercy, love—produce their own ferment. The man who has allowed these realities to come to him through the experience of suffering, in their own time and with their own priorities, knows that somehow and without any special action of his own initiative the ferment of these effects will be returned to the world in some form which is ultimately redemptive. He himself, henceforth and forever, if he has been deeply enough wounded, will remain reawakened to mercy and to that whole mysterious cycle of replenishment in which he has allowed himself to be used, to be an instrument, a filter.

Finally, to the sufferer's own great astonishment, he will experience within himself the effects of his mercy, effects that he never desired, never expected. This is what Gerald Vann understood so deeply when he wrote: "The merciful shall obtain more than they can desire. How is that? Because pity enlarges the heart, and where there is infinite pity, there is infinite enlargement of the heart, and so an infinite capacity for joy— and what that joy is, no man can tell."

—1969

Final Reflections

On Communication

Communication is the most tragic thing we've boggled, not only in the media but between people. When you look deeply into it you discover a latent racism. It's terrifying to see this racism developing in a country like Canada. I always hoped Canada would avoid the mistakes that we made in the United States. Yet these mistakes are repeated all over the world and they are essentially created by falsified communication.

First, there's the impediment of the double monologue — when whites are speaking without listening. A second source of dehumanization at work is using the Gospel to rationalize our prejudices and lack of charity. A third thing is a profound prior distrust in us that we have to recognize before we can finally believe that we are communicating at an authentic level. And fourth, whites must get away from this incredible longing to turn everybody else into pale imitations of themselves.

The deepest bitterness I find on the part of indigenous peoples in the Americas and in Canada is against early religious martyrs who tried to turn native peoples into white imitations. This is the same problem with black people and Christianity. How much longer are black people going to be missionary subjects?

This is always degrading and nobody's fooled by it.

Love does not possess but frees the other to be what he or she really is. The only way to freedom is not to try to make everybody else carbon copies of yourself. That's the history of missionary activity until recent years when we finally caught on that we do not insult people of another valid culture by trying to turn them into imitations of our culture.

The future is going to depend upon a kind of wisdom, but I don't know if that wisdom can come in time. Vast numbers of people are living in misery and are not preoccupied with wisdom.

I am not at all sure we can clean up basic communications to bring ourselves out of this frightened insularity in which most seem to be living in Canada and America.

Now I'm very preoccupied with things like the triage theory among the starving nations which says that since there's not going to be enough food for everyone, the ones who are starving can go ahead and starve so that the rest of us can eat. It is a terrible misuse of Darwinian thought.

It is a rebirth of an old idea really—stronger than we've seen it since the scientists under Hitler who rationalized the superiority of race. We now have what is called "academic racism" where even a Nobel prize winner contends people of color are intrinsically inferior intellectually.

Often I have been asked, "Can this process of racism be reversed?"

I was asked this once by a figure of world importance. When I told him yes, I still believed in that, he asked: "Then why couldn't we make all blacks white and solve this racial problem for good." He was serious.

I said, "Well, since three-fourths of the world's population is non-white, why not darken the one-fourth of us who are white?"

He quickly lost enthusiasm, and of course the whole idea of some of us making such decisions for others is a profound arrogance. Another error in his question is the idea, racist to the core, that all blacks would want to be white. The cure does not lie in changing color, but in the search for justice.

On Justice

The world has always been saved by an Abrahamic minority. There have always been a few who, in time of great trouble, become keenly aware of the underlying tragedy: the needless destruction of mankind.

This minority overdoes, gives every ounce, to compensate for the lack of awareness in the majority. This minority grows smaller, and when it disappears, it won't be the end of mankind. It will be the end of mankind as we know it.

There is an awful ethic of consensus which says that because this is a popular belief, let's base our ethics on it. Rule by majority is a great idea, but the majority has no right to rule wrongly based on prejudice. I can find five people right now whose consensus is that they should lynch me for being a traitor to the white race.

But that wouldn't make it right.

I've always been in the alleys of the world. You can't walk down an alley and see people suffering and keep walking. I learned early the horror of living other people's standards. Maybe one person could simply say: "To hell with success values," and live according to your conscience.

When I was blind I learned to type and wrote five books. People said it was extraordinary. But it was just that I refused to be put in a workshop. I resented very deeply the under challenging of the handicapped.

The greatest crime committed against the young is to under challenge them. In the early sixties, when we solicited the so-called "worthless" students to the South, you had extraordinary heroism. The young must be given the chance to have an early experience with ideals.

Nobody is more frustrated than people who reach maturity and are forced into retirement and a life of little significance. What a loss. It withers into lovelessness. Every time you love, it's a risk. That's why we have these words used in a bad way, like *sharing* or *witness*—these are words I gag on now, not because they're not magnificent words but because they've lost their significance. They've been trivialized. We take them like a dose of medicine.

We're not going to find the way out without some transcendence. Life is a risk. What a horror if you don't feel these risks. You end up being totally paralyzed. You don't ever do anything.

I have the kind of heart condition where if they catch me in the first nine minutes, they have a chance of saving me. If they can't, they don't. It's really fascinating, because I've always lived in danger. I just naturally have a feeling that I'm going to get through it.

The most distressing thing about this year of helplessness has been the terrible willingness of people to rush me to eternity. I'm not anxious to get rushed on. I want to live to the last moment.

Just before he died, J. Bronowski made one of the most electrifying remarks I ever heard: *Justice has now become a biological necessity in man*. It isn't a matter of choice, but a biological necessity. This is one of humanity's great unfinished themes.

On Dying

As I approach the end of life I become enormously preoccupied with the quality of life and with what people do for each other. You gain a perspective toward the end that leaves you with one source of grief—all the time you spent selfishly when you could have done something for somebody else.

I write as much as I've got strength to write, but I've been fascinated with the difference between the things we say about dying and the reality of dying. This has been a revelation to me. So the little writing that I am doing is really more or less keeping journal notes on how utterly unreal are most things people say and most advice they give on the subject.

About dying, I can say only what I have always said about people in physical pain or with any kind of a handicap. It is the attitude of others that kills you finally. There are a great many doctors who would put me in the hospital where I would die very quickly, because now I have to live a life with as little stress as possible.

When I get cards from religious people saying, "Alleluia, soon you'll be with your Maker," they seem overjoyed at the fact that I'm not very far from this. Suddenly it doesn't seem real anymore. I have the feeling that people have written all these things about death and dying out of great fear of it themselves, and what they have written is not really true.

On the other hand, the most damaging people are the ones who come in and give me pep talks, who advise me to do this and to do that, and who bring me books which say that a heart patient ought to recover. I received one like that not too long ago. It said that in order to recover from this kind of heart disease I should eat the berries from laurel trees, flax seeds, okra and jog briskly as far as I can each day. To follow this advice I'd be dead in five minutes. My own doctor, who's a very good heart specialist, tells me to move like a snail.

But there's still a shattering readjustment that one has to make. I don't know how other people work on faith but for me it was an almost existential choice. There was no other way to go many years ago. I tried to do the will of God as well as I could and the first thing I discovered was that this didn't automatically make me a lover of God.

The second thing I discovered is that most often people interpret the will of God through their own desires. I found that never really worked for me; the will of God rarely coincided with any desire of mine!

And toward the end, I've come to the realization that all that I believe was right and all of it was truth. That I was right about the reality of faith. That's been an extraordinary revelation to me, because I am very often dealing with people who are struggling or who are young or attached to life and who want ten million guarantees beforehand. It just doesn't work this way. And then I deal with people who have based their lives on doing God's will without ever knowing that God's will is a matter of faith, not of doing what you want.

That's where the immense consolation comes to me, to find out that I've gambled and that the gamble was right. But what people don't really know is that a long time before I made the *Black Like Me* experiment I took another great gamble—what the French call simply *le grand oui*, the great yes. The gamble was for God. That means leaping off that cliff and never knowing where you're going to land, but you the faith that you're going to land somewhere. That was my conversion to Roman Catholicism. But it was more than that for me. I took the initial gamble but it's not one that lasts. I go through reconversion every day.

We say things with a great deal too much facility about suffering. I think of Jacques and Raïssa Maritain who were both very deeply afflicted by the Hitler era. Raïssa was originally Jewish and took on herself the pains and sufferings of the Jewish people. She was in agony for many years, one physical suffering after another. She said that if people can use the suffering, if they can learn from it, then it is infinitely valuable. If they can't learn from it, suffering is of no use whatsoever.

One thing people have to learn is that the suffering person has to become the consoler. Suffering people must always be preoccupied with the misery that they are causing those who love them. The second thing people learn from suffering is that if you can suffer without a hint of self-pity, then this develops an almost limitless capacity for compassion. Most people bend and break, "Why me, O Lord?" This "poor me" attitude suffocates you to death. It breaks you. What you have to learn to do is to handle it. It's real, it's there; sometimes it is so "there" it is paralyzing.

That thought came to me as a kind of light when I was blinded. For about six months I had no usable vision. I could see forms coming at me but I didn't know what they were. That was an agony. It was a great relief to pass from that stage to total loss of vision.

But every one asked: "Do you feel bitter about this?"

I would think to myself, if it hadn't been me it would have been one of my longtime army friends. I could not help to be glad it happened to me and not one of them. How could I wish this on anybody else?

So suffering can work that way. When I lost my sight, there wasn't any brain surgery that could correct it. The doctor, who was a great neurosurgeon, told me that I would be completely without sight in six months, to forget surgery and start adjusting my life. It's the best thing he could have done.

Regaining sight was far more difficult than losing it, because the sight overwhelmed every other sense. I had married in the meantime and had a wife and children I'd never seen.

Since I was nineteen, I have been thrown into situations I never intended or chose, which always led to helping people who were victims of inhumane treatment. These experiences sear you forever.

Acknowledgments

All rights to John Howard Griffin's works are controlled by The Estate of John Howard Griffin and Elizabeth Griffin-Bonazzi.

Studs Terkel's *Remembrance* and Robert Bonazzi's *Introduction* appear here for the first time.

"Privacy of Conscience" was adapted from interviews in *Latitudes* magazine, 1966-1967. Griffin's remarks were made to editors Daniel L. Robertson and Bonazzi, who first visited the author in Mansfield, Texas, in 1966.

"The Intrinsic *Other*" was written in French and published in *Building Peace*, edited by Nobel Peace Laureate Dominique Pire (1966). The first edition appeared in Belgium and France. Griffin translated the essay into English and it was published in *The John Howard Griffin Reader*, edited by Bradford Daniel (Houghton Mifflin, 1968).

"Profile of A Racist" first appeared as "Profile of a Bigot" in *Encounters With the Other* (Latitudes Press, 1997).

The review of *Killers of the Dream* was published in *Southwest Review* magazine, in 1962. Excerpts from the letters of Lillian Smith and the journals of John Howard Griffin in the *Introduction* are published here for the first time.

"Requiem for A Martyr" appeared in *The Progressive* magazine in 1964, as an interview with Bradford Daniel; this edited version was reprinted in *Encounters With the Other*.

"Racist Sins of Christians" first appeared in *Sign* magazine in 1963 and was reprinted in *The John Howard Griffin Reader*.

"Malcolm X" appeared in *Sepia* magazine in 1975, and is reprinted here for the first time in book form.

The texts from "American Racism in the Sixties" are excerpted from *The Church and the Black Man* (Pflaum Press, 1969) and the monograph *On Our Doorstep* (Pio Decimo Press, 1967).

A Time To Be Human was Griffin's final book on racism (Macmillan, New York, and Collier Macmillan, London, 1977).

"Poulenc Behind the Mask" first appeared in *Ramparts* magazine in 1965 and was reprinted in the *John Howard Griffin Reader.*

"Fraternal Dialogue" first appeared under the title "A Visit to Huy" in *Ramparts* magazine in 1965 and was reprinted in *The John Howard Griffin Reader.*

"The Little Brothers" was first published in *Ramparts* magazine in 1965; it appears here for the first time in book form.

"The Terrain of Physical Pain" was written in Thomas Merton's hermitage in 1969 and first published in the anthology, *Creative Suffering*, edited by James F. Andrews (Pilgrim Press, 1970).

"Final Reflections" was adapted from a 1978 interview with Studs Terkel that first appeared in Terkel's book of interviews, *American Dreams: Lost and Found* (Pantheon, 1980), and in an interview with Thurston Smith in *US Catholic* magazine in 1977.

About the Editor

The Scribbling Cure: Poems and Prose Poems (Pecan Grove Press, 2011) and *Maestro of Solitude: Poems and Poetics* (Wings, 2007) constitute a selected volume, 1970-2010. Earlier books *Living the Borrowed Life* (1974), *Fictive Music: Prose Poems* (1979) and *Perpetual Texts* (1986), were praised by Mark Van Doren, Thomas Merton, Guy Davenport, Vassar Miller, Naomi Shihab Nye, Paul Christensen, Robert Peters and others.

Man in the Mirror: John Howard Griffin and the Story of Black Like Me (Orbis, 1997) was praised by Jonathan Kozol, Studs Terkel, *The Times of London, Chicago Tribune, Library Journal, National Catholic Reporter, Publishers Weekly, The Catholic Worker, Booklist, Texas Observer, Texas Books in Review* and *Multicultural Review*. As Literary Executor for The Estate of John Howard Griffin, Bonazzi has written introductions and afterwords to Griffin's *Black Like Me, Scattered Shadows: A Memoir of Blindness and Vision, Available Light: Exile in Mexico, Follow the Ecstasy: The Hermitage Years of Thomas Merton, Street of the Seven Angels* and *Encounters With the Other*. His work on Griffin has appeared in *The New York Times, Bloomsbury Review* and *The Historical Dictionary of Civil Rights*. Bonazzi's creative and critical work has been published in over 200 publications—in France, Germany, Japan, South Korea, Canada, Mexico, Peru and the U.K. He appears in the documentary, *Uncommon Vision: The Life and Times of John Howard* Griffin (produced by Morgan Atkinson and aired on PBS).

Born in New York City in 1942, Bonazzi has also lived in Mexico City, Florida, San Francisco and several Texas cities. From 1966-2000, he edited and published over 100 titles under his Latitudes imprint. He lives in San Antonio and writes a column on poetry for the *San Antonio Express-News* and reviews for *World Literature Today*.

Wings Press was founded in 1975 by Joanie Whitebird and Joseph F. Lomax, both deceased, as "an informal association of artists and cultural mythologists dedicated to the preservation of the literature of the nation of Texas." Publisher, editor and designer since 1995, Bryce Milligan is honored to carry on and expand that mission to include the finest in American writing—meaning all of the Americas, without commercial considerations clouding the choice to publish or not to publish.

Wings Press produces multicultural books, chapbooks, CDs, DVDs and broadsides that, we hope, enlighten the human spirit and enliven the mind. Everyone ever associated with Wings has been or is a writer, and we know well that writing is a transformational art form capable of changing the world, primarily by allowing us to glimpse something of each other's souls. Good writing is innovative, insightful, and interesting. But most of all it is honest.

Likewise, Wings Press is committed to treating the planet itself as a partner. Thus the press uses as much recycled material as possible, from the paper on which the books are printed to the boxes in which they are shipped.

As Robert Dana wrote in *Against the Grain*, "Small press publishing is personal publishing. In essence, it's a matter of personal vision, personal taste and courage, and personal friendships." Welcome to our world.

Colophon

The Wings Press cloth edition of *Prison of Culture:
Beyond Black Like Me*, by John Howard Griffin, edited
and introduced by Robert Bonazzi, is printed on 70
pound non-acidic Arbor paper by Edwards Brothers,
Inc. of Ann Arbor, Michigan. Text and interior titles
are set in Cochin type. All Wings Press books are
designed by Bryce Milligan.

On-line catalogue and ordering:
www.wingspress.com

Wings Press titles are distributed
to the trade by the
Independent Publishers Group
www.ipgbook.com
and in Europe by
www.gazellebookservices.co.uk